A Tale of Two Cities

CHARLES DICKENS

Level 5

Retold by A. Johnson and G. C. Thornley
Series Editors: Andy Hopkins and Jocelyn Potter

Pearson Education Limited
Edinburgh Gate, Harlow,
Essex CM20 2JE, England
and Associated Companies throughout the world.

ISBN: 978-1-4058-6256-1

First published in the Longman Simplified English Series 1947
First published in the Longman Fiction Series 1993
This adaptation first published in 1996
First Penguin Books edition published 1999
This edition published 2008

3 5 7 9 10 8 6 4 2

Text copyright © Penguin Books Ltd 1999
This edition copyright © Pearson Education Ltd 2008

Typeset by Graphicraft Ltd, Hong Kong
Set in 11/14pt Bembo
Printed in China
SWTC/02

Published by Pearson Education Ltd in association with
Penguin Books Ltd, both companies being subsidiaries of Pearson Plc

For a complete list of the titles available in the Penguin Readers series please write to your local
Pearson Longman office or to: Penguin Readers Marketing Department, Pearson Education,
Edinburgh Gate, Harlow, Essex CM20 2JE, England.

Contents

Introduction

The new age began; the King was tried and put to death; the black flag waved from the great towers of Notre-Dame (the most important church in Paris); the prisons were filled with people who had done no wrong; and the guillotine struck down the powerful and killed the beautiful and the good. Among all these terrors walked the Doctor with a steady head, never doubting that he would save Lucie's husband in the end.

A Tale of Two Cities takes place against the exciting background of the French Revolution. The story begins in 1775. Dr Manette, a French doctor, has been a prisoner in the terrible Bastille prison for many years. He is found, half crazy, by his daughter Lucie and Mr Lorry, who have gone to Paris to search for him. They take him back to London, where his health and his memory gradually improve. Five years later, the Frenchman Charles Darnay is tried in London on charges of spying. He is freed, partly because he is very similar in appearance to the lawyer Sydney Carton; this similarity becomes even more important later in the story. Both Darnay and Carton are in love with Lucie. At the same time, the Revolution is starting in France. Darnay is forced to put his own life in danger by going back there to help the tax collector, Gabelle. Darnay is followed by Lucie and Dr Manette, who is now fully recovered, and plays an important part in the exciting events that follow.

A Tale of Two Cities (1859) is the second of the two works of historical fiction written by Charles Dickens and is one of his most popular novels. Like many of his stories, it was originally written and sold one part at a time, and the book depends less on character for its interest than on the excitement of the developing tale. In the story, Dickens uses his famous skills as a descriptive writer to paint a powerful picture of the French Revolution in all its madness and horror. His scenes of angry crowds have been described as 'staying in the mind forever'. Against this background, Dickens tells a stirring love story. Two men love the same woman. One of them wins her. The other, although he knows he will never have her, does something extraordinarily heroic to make the woman he loves happy. For these reasons, *A Tale of Two Cities* is of the author's most unforgettable novels.

Charles Dickens, one of Britain's greatest novelists, was born in Portsmouth, England, in 1812 and moved to London with his family when he was about two years old. The family was very poor, and John Dickens, a clerk with the navy, could not earn enough to support his wife and eight children. Charles, the second oldest, attended school for a time and one of his schoolteachers recognised his talent and gave him particular attention. However, his school education did not last long, since the family's situation forced him to leave school. Two days after his twelfth birthday, Dickens was sent to work in a shoe polish factory. At about the same time, his father was sent to prison as a debtor.

The difficulties the family suffered and the general hopelessness he saw around him as he was growing up shaped Dickens's view of the world; the subject of poverty and its effects featured greatly in his later writing. Determined to leave behind the troubles of his childhood, Dickens started writing for a newspaper. By the age of twenty he was known as a reporter in London's law courts and at the House of Commons.

Dickens then started writing short pieces for monthly magazines. His first success as a novelist came with the appearance, in monthly parts, of *The Pickwick Papers*, when he was twenty-four. The novel made him famous and wealthy.

However, while he was successful in public life, Dickens's personal life was not happy. He married Catherine Hogarth in 1836 and they had ten children together. As time passed they became increasingly unhappy, and they separated in 1858. By then, Dickens had fallen in love with a clever and charming young actress called Ellen Ternan. When they first met, Dickens was forty-five and Ellen was eighteen. The couple continued their relationship until the novelist's death, although the relationship had to remain secret as the public would have been very shocked if it had been discovered.

Dickens was a man of enormous energy. As well as writing twenty full-length fictional stories and many works of non-fiction, he found the time to work for a number of organizations that helped the poor. This concern for people and social conditions is characteristic of much of Dickens's work. He also did tours of England and the United States, giving popular theatrical readings of his best-known novels. Under the pressure of these activities his health grew worse, and he died suddenly in 1870.

Dickens had all the qualities needed for a great novelist. He was a keen observer of people and places, had a great understanding of human nature, and was particularly sympathetic towards young people. He was at his best describing memorable characters and scenes which were typical of life in mid-nineteenth-century London. His stories demand the reader's interest and are full of humour and a sense of life.

Oliver Twist (1837–9) tells of the adventures of a poor, unloved child in London's criminal class, while the cruelty of the private school system is attacked in *Nicholas Nickleby* (another early story). During the 1840s, Dickens wrote five 'Christmas books'. The first of these, *A Christmas Carol*, tells the story of rich, mean Ebenezer Scrooge who, late in life, learns the meaning of Christmas and discovers happiness by helping others people who are less fortunate than himself. *David Copperfield* (1850) is based partly on Dickens's childhood, and was described by him as his favourite child. It is the story of a young man's childhood and growth to adulthood.

In his later works, including *Hard Times*, *Little Dorrit* and *Our Mutual Friend*, Dickens presents a much darker view of the world. His humour is used to attack the evil side of human experience; in particular, the inhuman social effects of industry and trade.

Bleak House shows the unfairness of the legal system and how lawyers could lengthen the legal process. In the novel they do this for their own financial gain, without any concern for the damage done to the lives of the people involved in their cases. However, *Great Expectations*, also written during this period, is not as dark as the other novels. Instead, there is a journey of discovery as the hero, Pip, tells readers how he tries to achieve his 'great expectations' and instead discovers real human values.

To understand *A Tale of Two Cities*, it helps to know something about its background of the French Revolution. France, at the time of the Revolution, was a country in which the King, Louis XVI, was extremely powerful. The King, the royal family and the aristocracy were very rich, and their wealth came from the high taxes that they demanded of ordinary French people, who were becoming increasingly poor. The people became more and more discontented and angry, and in May 1789 the government tried to place some controls on the power of the King.

However, the King refused to accept any controls and on 14 July 1789 a violent crowd succeeded in entering the terrible Bastille prison in Paris and freeing the prisoners. On 20 June 1791, the royal family attempted to escape but were brought back. On 10 August, an angry crowd entered the royal palace and on 21 September the First French Republic officially began. Then on 21 January 1793, Louis XVI was put to death on the guillotine.

In June the control of the country passed to a group called the Committee of Public Safety, led by Robespierre. Over the next year, as many as 40,000 aristocrats and other more ordinary people were imprisoned and put to death on the guillotine, often for no good reason. This terrible time is brilliantly described in Dickens's novel. In July 1794, the Committee and Robespierre were replaced by a less extreme form of government, which ruled until Napoleon seized power in 1799.

In *A Tale of Two Cities*, Dickens shows the causes of the Revolution and its effects on people's daily lives. The historical detail of the book is based on the great work *The French Revolution*, by Dickens's friend Thomas Carlyle. Dickens himself made many journeys to Paris, and visited the remaining historical sights of the Revolution. Britain in Dickens's time was socially much less settled than it is today, and many people felt that there was a danger of a popular rebellion against the wealthier classes. They therefore took a great interest in the lessons that could be learned from the French experience.

Dickens, as is clear from the book, had two very contrasting attitudes to the Revolution. He was very sympathetic towards the poor and their treatment by the aristocracy; in the novel, the aristocrat the Marquis* of Evrémonde is shown to be a cruel man who does not care about the suffering of the poor. However, Dickens was also shocked by the violence of the crowds and their pleasure when people were killed on the guillotine. In the novel, Madame Defarge is an example of a type of French woman who existed at that time and whose one desire was to see aristocrats die.

Dickens described himself as caring greatly about *A Tale of Two Cities*. This was partly because of his interest in the French Revolution, but also because at the time of writing he was hopelessly in love with Ellen Ternan, while still living with his wife. In Sydney Carton's desperate love for Lucie Manette he

---

* **Marquis**: the title a man from a high-class French family

ix

saw a parallel with his own love for Ellen – a woman whom he loved but believed he could never have. It has been suggested that Carton's final action at the end of the book was Dickens's way of imagining what he himself would do for Ellen if he had to. Carton's last words, which are so famous, are an unforgettable statement of the power of love.

Chapter 1   The Shop of Monsieur* Defarge

Saint-Antoine was one of the poorest parts of Paris. The children who lived there had the faces and sad voices of old men, and hunger seemed to be written on the face of every man and woman. The shops contained only the worst bits of meat and only the cheapest loaves. Nothing brightened the streets except the shops that sold tools or weapons; these contained the sharpest of bright knives and the most murderous of guns, shining weapons which seemed to be waiting for the time when they would be brought out to do terrible work.

A large barrel of wine had been dropped and broken in one of the streets of Saint-Antoine. Red wine began to run over the rough stones. Little pools of it formed in the hollows and cracks among the stones.

Immediately, everyone left whatever they were doing, and ran to the spot to collect some of the wine before it disappeared into the ground. Some knelt down and tried to drink it from their hands, but most of it ran through their fingers. Some brought cups and tried to fill them; others dipped cloths in the wine and then put them in their mouths. For a time, in that street of poor and miserable people, the joyful sound of laughter rang out. But soon all the wine was gone; the laughter died down and the people returned to what they had been doing before.

A tall man dipped his finger in some mud made red with the wine and wrote on the wall five big letters: BLOOD. The time would come when blood would flow in the streets of Saint-Antoine and would turn its stones red again.

The barrel of wine had been on its way to the wine shop at

* **Monsieur, Madame**: the French words for Mr/sir and Mrs/madam

the corner. Outside stood the owner of the shop, Monsieur Defarge.

He was a strongly built man of about thirty, with a face that was good-natured on the whole, but which showed signs of strong determination and a complete absence of any kind of weakness. He was a man who would be an enemy to be feared.

Monsieur Defarge stood looking at the struggle for the wine for some time. 'It isn't my affair,' he said to himself. 'As that barrel is broken, they must bring me another.' Then his eye caught sight of the man who had written the terrible word on the wall. He called to him: 'Say, Gaspard, are you crazy? Why do you write in the public street? Are there no better places to write such words?'

Madame Defarge was sitting in the shop when her husband re-entered it. She was a woman of about his own age, with a very keen eye, a strong face and a great calmness of manner. As her husband came in, she gave a little cough and looked in a certain direction as if to call his attention to some people who had just come into the shop.

The shopkeeper looked around until his eye rested on an oldish gentleman and a young woman who were seated in a corner. There were other people in the shop, but only these two were strangers. As he passed he noticed that the old man attracted the attention of his young companion as if to say, 'This is our man'.

'What on earth are those two doing there?' said Defarge to himself. 'I don't know them.'

He pretended not to notice the two strangers, and fell into a conversation with three men who were drinking at the bar.

'How goes it, Jacques?' said one of them to Monsieur Defarge. 'Is all the wine drunk from the broken barrel?'

'Every drop of it, Jacques,' replied Defarge.

'It isn't often,' said the second man, 'that these miserable creatures know the taste of wine, or of anything but black bread and death. Isn't that so, Jacques?'

2

'It is so, Jacques,' replied Monsieur Defarge.

The third man put down his glass.

'Ah! Such poor cattle always have a bitter taste in their mouths; they lead a hard life. Am I right, Jacques?'

'You are right, Jacques,' replied Monsieur Defarge.

A movement from Madame Defarge attracted his attention. 'Gentlemen,' he said, 'the room that you wish to see is at the top of the stairs. Go into the courtyard. One of you has been there before and will show you the way.'

They paid for their wine and left. The oldish gentleman walked towards Monsieur Defarge and asked permission to speak to him. Their conversation was short. Almost at the first word Monsieur Defarge's face showed keen attention. After a minute Defarge signalled his agreement and went out. The gentleman then called to the young lady, and they, too, went outside.

Madame went on with her knitting and took no notice.

Mr Jarvis Lorry (the gentleman) and Miss Lucie Manette joined Defarge in the courtyard to which he had recently directed the three men. In the courtyard Defarge did a surprising thing. He went down on one knee and put his lips to the young lady's hand.

Defarge at one time had been a servant of Dr Manette, Lucie's father. Lucie's mother had died, and her father had disappeared: no one knew what had happened to him. His money was in Tellson's Bank – an English bank. The baby Lucie was brought to England, and Mr Jarvis Lorry, an official of Tellson's Bank and an old friend of her father's, was put in charge of her money and her education. Mr Lorry had asked an Englishwoman, Miss Pross, to bring up the child. Over the years that followed, Miss Pross became like a mother to Lucie and would have given her life for her.

Lucie was now a young woman, and strange news had brought her and Mr Lorry to Paris – news that Dr Manette (who all had thought to be dead) was alive. He had been a prisoner in the Bastille, the great prison of Paris. Now he had been set free and was in the care of his old servant, Defarge.

Defarge rose to his feet. A remarkable change had come over his face. A look of anger and hatred had replaced his good-natured expression – hatred for those who had harmed someone he loved,

'The stairs are high,' said Defarge. 'Let us go up slowly.'

'Is Dr Manette alone?' whispered Mr Lorry.

'Of course. He has been used to being alone for so long that now he cannot bear the presence of others.'

'Is he greatly changed?'

'Changed! You will not recognize him.'

As they neared the top of the stairs, Defarge took a key out of his pocket.

'Do you keep his door locked?'

'I think it safer to do so.'

'Why?'

'Why! Because he has lived so long locked up that he would be frightened if his door was left open.'

'Is it possible?' asked Mr Lorry in surprise.

'It is possible,' replied Defarge bitterly. 'In this beautiful world such things are possible, and not only possible, they are actually done every day. Such is the state of France.'

This conversation had been held in so low a whisper that none of it reached the young lady's ears, but as they neared the top of the stairs she was shaking. Her face showed such deep anxiety, such terror, that Mr Lorry spoke to her to calm her.

'Courage, my dear! Courage! The worst will be over in a minute. Think only of the happiness you will bring him.'

As last they were near the top. Suddenly, at a turn in the stairs, they came upon the three men who were looking into a room through the cracks in a door. Hearing footsteps they turned and rose: they were the three men who had been drinking in the wine shop.

'Leave us, boys. We have business here,' said Defarge.

The three went quietly down.

Mr Lorry was angry. He whispered to Defarge, 'Do you make a show of Monsieur Manette?'

'I show him to a few, to those to whom the sight is likely to do good. They are all men of my own name, Jacques. You are English and do not understand. Stay here a minute, please.'

Defarge ran his key along the door as if to give a warning to the person inside. Then he put it in the lock and turned it slowly. The door opened; he looked into the room and said something. A faint voice answered. Defarge looked back and signalled to them to enter. Mr Lorry put his arm round Lucie's waist and held her. 'Go in,' he said. 'Go in.'

'I am afraid,' she answered, still shaking.

'Afraid of what?'

'I am afraid of him, my father.'

He pulled her arm around his neck, lifted her a little and hurried into the room.

Work was going on in the room. With his back towards the door and his face towards the window, a white-haired man sat on a long bench, bent forward. He was very busy, making shoes.

Chapter 2   The Shoemaker

'Good day,' said Monsieur Defarge, looking down at the white head.

The white head was raised for a moment. Then a faint voice replied, 'Good day.'

'You are still hard at work, I see.'

After a long silence the head was lifted again for a moment

and the weak voice replied, 'Yes – I am still working.'

The faintness of the voice was pitiful. It seemed to be the result not only of bodily weakness but also of lack of practice. The old man was poorly dressed. He had a white beard, a hollow face and extremely bright eyes that appeared to be unnaturally large. He took no notice of his visitors; he hardly seemed to know that they were there. His mind had obviously been affected by the long years in prison.

Mr Lorry came silently forward, leaving Lucie by the door.

'Come,' said Defarge, 'you have a visitor. Show him the shoe that you are making. Tell him what kind of a shoe it is.'

The weak voice replied, 'It is a lady's shoe, a young lady's shoe. It is in the present fashion. But I have never seen such a shoe. I have only seen a pattern.' He looked at the shoe with a little pride, pride in his own work.

'And what is your name?' asked Mr Lorry.

'My name? One Hundred and Five, North Tower.'

'What? Is that all?'

'One Hundred and Five, North Tower.'

'But you are not a shoemaker by trade, are you?' asked Mr Lorry.

The old man paused for a while. 'No,' he said, 'I am not a shoemaker by trade. I learned it in prison. They gave me permission to learn.'

Mr Lorry looked steadily into his face.

'Dr Manette, don't you remember me?'

The shoe dropped to the ground. The old man looked in wonder at his questioner.

'Dr Manette, don't you remember Monsieur Defarge here? Don't you remember Jarvis Lorry, the old banker?'

The prisoner of many years looked from one to the other. A look of intelligence seemed to come over his face. Then it disappeared again. Darkness clouded his mind. He picked up the shoe and continued his work.

Slowly, very slowly, Lucie drew near the bench of the shoemaker. She stood beside him as he bent over his work.

He dropped his knife, bent down to pick it up, and caught sight of her dress. He looked at her closely and breathed heavily. The two men were afraid; he had the knife in his hand and she was very near him. But she showed no sign of fear.

'Who are you? Are you the prison guard's daughter?'

'No,' she whispered.

'Who are you?'

She could not speak, but she sat down beside him on the bench. He moved away from her, but she laid her hand on his arm. He dropped his knife and sat looking at her.

Her golden hair lay in curls on her shoulders. Nervously he put out his hand to touch it. Then he breathed deeply and went on with his shoemaking.

Again the old man stopped; he touched Lucie's hair once more and looked closely at it.

'It is the same,' he said. 'But how can it be?'

He put his hand to his neck and took off a blackened string that had a folded piece of cloth at the end of it. He opened this, carefully, on his knee. It contained a small quantity of hair – hairs which he had carefully saved long, long ago.

He took her hair in his hand again.

'It is the same. But how can it be? She laid her head upon my shoulder that night when I was called out. And when I was brought to the North Tower I found these hairs on my coat.'

He turned to her with frightening suddenness. But she sat perfectly still and, when Defarge and Mr Lorry wanted to come to her help, only said, 'I beg you, gentlemen, do not come near us, do not speak, do not move.'

'Whose voice is that?' he cried. 'What is your name?'

'Oh, sir, at another time you shall hear my name, and who my

7

mother was, and who my father. But I cannot tell you now, and I cannot tell you here. All that I can tell you is that I love you, and that I beg you to kiss me.'

She put her arm round his neck and held his head to her breast as if he were a child.

'Thank God your long sorrow is over. From here we are going to England to be at peace and at rest. Rest, rest. Give thanks to God, who has brought you through so much suffering into peace at last.'

For a long time he remained with her arm around him. Then he slipped softly to the floor. A great calm had followed the storm. He slept as peacefully as a child.

Mr Lorry bent over the sleeping man. 'We must take him away now, immediately.'

'But is he fit for the journey?' said Lucie.

'Fitter for the journey than to remain in this city, so terrible to him.'

'It is true,' said Defarge. 'And for many reasons Monsieur Manette would be better out of France. Say, shall I hire a carriage and horses?'

'That is business,' said Mr Lorry. 'And if business is to be done, I am the man to do it.'

'Then please leave us here,' said Lucie. 'You see how quiet he has become. Lock the door when you go out. Leave us together. Do not be afraid. He is quite safe with me, and I am quite safe with him.'

The two men went away to make arrangements for the journey. When they had gone, the daughter sat and watched her father. The darkness deepened and deepened. He lay quiet until a light shone through the cracks in the door. It was time to leave.

As one long used to being given orders, he ate and drank what they gave him, put on the clothes they had brought for him, and went with them. Lucie put her arm through his. He

8

took her hand in both of his own and kept it there. They began to go down the stairs.

There was no crowd near the wine shop to see them go. Only one person was to be seen, and that was Madame Defarge, who leaned against the doorpost, knitting, and seemed to notice nothing.

Chapter 3   The Trial

Tellson's Bank in London was an old-fashioned place even in 1780. It was very small, very dark and very ugly, but the owners were proud of its smallness, its darkness and its ugliness; they thought that if it looked better, it would be less respectable. Inside its honourable walls, the only men to be seen, carrying on its business with great seriousness, were very old; it was believed that if a young man joined the bank, they hid him until he was old enough to be seen.

One March morning, five years after Dr Manette came to London, one of the oldest of the clerks in the bank sent for Jeremy Cruncher, the messenger, who usually spent his time sitting just outside the door.

'Do you know the court of justice called the Old Bailey?' asked the old clerk.

'Ye-es, sir,' said Jerry anxiously.

'And you know Mr Lorry?'

'Much better than I know the Old Bailey, sir.'

'Very well. Go to the doorkeeper of the court and show him this note for Mr Lorry. He will then let you in. When you are inside, show yourself to Mr Lorry and wait until he asks for you.'

Jerry took the letter, and set out for the Old Bailey. As he came near, he had to make his way through a crowd of people, all attracted to the place by the coming trial and hoping to see the accused man. All the doors were guarded, but when Jerry showed the letter, one of the doors was opened to let him in.

'What's the next case?' Jerry asked a man near him.

'Charles Darnay – the man accused of helping the King's enemies.'

Mr Cruncher saw the doorkeeper go to Mr Lorry with the note in his hand. Mr Lorry was sitting among the lawyers at a table in the courtroom. One of these lawyers was Mr Stryver; he was appearing for Darnay, and had a lot of papers in front of him. Nearly opposite was another gentleman whose whole attention seemed to be fixed on the ceiling. When Mr Lorry saw Cruncher, he signalled quietly to him.

The entrance of the judge stopped all the talking. Then the prisoner was led in. Everyone looked in his direction – except one man, the carelessly dressed man who sat looking at the ceiling. Sydney Carton was his name.

The prisoner was a young man of about twenty-five; he seemed to be a gentleman. He was quite calm and lowered his head politely to the judge.

There was silence in the court. Charles Darnay had the day before sworn that he was not guilty. But he was here accused of being a spy and of helping Louis, the French king, in his wars against the King of England. He was accused of travelling between England and France, and informing the French of the armies that the King of England was making ready to send to Canada and North America.

The accused man listened to all this calmly; but as he did so he looked around the court and noticed two persons on his left. When his eyes fell on them, his appearance changed so greatly that the attention of everyone in the court was directed towards them. They were a young lady of little more than twenty, and a gentleman with very white hair who was clearly her father. His daughter, Lucie, had one of her hands through the old man's arm and was looking at the prisoner with great pity. From the crowd around him, Jerry learned that they were witnesses against the prisoner.

The government lawyer rose to open the case against Darnay. 'This prisoner,' he said, 'is in the habit of travelling between England and France on business. What this business is might not have been discovered, but fortunately an honest man, John Barsad, who was at one time the prisoner's friend, found out, and Roger Cly, the prisoner's servant, discovered papers in the prisoner's pockets and in his room. On these papers were lists of the English armies and their positions. It cannot be proved that these lists are written in the prisoner's handwriting, but,' said the lawyer, 'this shows that the prisoner is a clever and imaginative man who has tried in this way to cover up his actions.'

First John Barsad gave evidence of these facts. He was then questioned by Mr Stryver, who was defending Charles Darnay:

'Have you ever been a spy?'

'Certainly not.'

'Have you ever been in prison?'

'No.'

'Never in a debtors' prison?'

'I don't see what that has to do with it.'

'Come! Never in a debtors' prison?'

'Yes.'

'How often?'

'Two or three times.'

'Have you ever been accused of dishonesty?'

'It was only in a game of cards. They said so – but they were drunk.'

'Are you sure you know the prisoner well?'

'Yes.'

'Do you expect to be paid for giving evidence?'

'Certainly not!'

Roger Cly came next. He said that he had often seen such lists when arranging the prisoner's clothes; he had found the lists (shown in court) in the prisoner's room. He had seen the prisoner show the lists to a Frenchman at Calais. Questioned by Mr Stryver, Roger Cly admitted that he had once been a thief.

Then came Mr Lorry. He was asked whether he had seen the prisoner before, and replied that he had seen him board a ship at Calais.

'At what time did he come on board?'

'At a little after midnight.'

'Were you travelling alone, Mr Lorry?'

'I was with two others. A gentleman and a lady. They are here.'

'Miss Manette!'

The young lady towards whom all eyes had been turned before stood up.

'Miss Manette, look at the prisoner.'

It had been difficult for Charles Darnay to stand before that crowd in the court, but until now he had seemed calm and unmoved. But faced by the youth and beauty – and pity – of Lucie Manette, his lips shook.

'Miss Manette, have you seen the prisoner before?'

'Yes, sir.'

'Where?'

'On board the ship just mentioned.'

'Did you speak to the prisoner?'

'When he came on board, he noticed that my father was very tired and weak. He was kind enough to help me shelter my father from the wind and the weather.'

'Did he come on board alone?'

'No.'

'How many came with him?'

'Two French gentlemen.'

'Were any papers handed about among them, like these lists?'

'Some papers were, but I don't know what papers.'

'What did the prisoner say to you?'

'He was kind and good, and helpful to my father.' At this point the witness burst into tears. 'I hope I may not repay him by doing him harm today.'

'Everyone understands, Miss Manette, that you are appearing in court against your will, because it is your duty. Please go on.'

'He told me that he was travelling on business of a delicate kind and was therefore using a false name. He said that he might have to travel between France and England quite often in the future.'

'Did he say anything about America?'

'He tried to explain how that quarrel had started, and he thought that England was in the wrong. He added jokingly that George Washington might be as famous in history as George the Third.'

The judge looked up from his notes in surprise and anger at these words, and all the people in court noticed the anxiety of the witness as she said them.

Dr Manette was then called and asked if he had seen the prisoner before.

'Once, when he came to see me in London.'

'Did he travel with you in the ship?'

'I cannot say.'

'Is there any special reason why you cannot?'

'There is.'

'Has it been your misfortune to suffer a long period in prison without trial or accusation, in your own country?'

'A long period in prison.'

'Were you at that time only recently set free?'

'They tell me so.'

'But you remember nothing?'

'Nothing between the time when I used to make shoes in prison, and the time when I found myself living in London with my dear daughter.'

A witness was then called who said that he had seen the prisoner in a hotel in a town where there was a shipyard and a soldiers' camp. The lawyers were trying to prove that he had gone there to obtain valuable information.

Sydney Carton had all this time seemed to be taking no notice: he had just been sitting there, looking at the ceiling. But now he wrote a few words on a piece of paper and threw it to Mr Stryver. After examining it, Mr Stryver said to the witness:

'Are you quite sure that it was the prisoner?'

'Quite sure.'

'Have you ever seen anyone like the prisoner?'

'Not so like him that I could be mistaken.'

'Look well at that gentleman, over there,' said Stryver, pointing to the man who had thrown him the paper. 'Do you think he is like the prisoner?'

Although the man was dirty and careless in his appearance, and was dressed as a lawyer, everyone in the courtroom was surprised by the likeness.

'If a man so like the prisoner could be found by chance in this court, another man, just as like him, might chance to be in that hotel,' said Mr Stryver.

So the evidence was worthless.

There were no more witnesses to be heard, and the lawyers' closing speeches were made. The judge made his remarks. The 12 men of the jury then left the court to consider their decision.

Mr Carton must have noticed more of what was going on than he appeared to do; for, when Miss Manette fainted, he was the first to cry out.

'Officer, help the gentlemen to take that young lady out of

the court! Don't you see that she will fall?'

The prisoner seemed to be much affected by the trouble he had caused Miss Manette, and asked Mr Carton to tell her that he was sorry to be the cause of her unhappiness.

The jury were absent for an hour and a half, during which time Jerry Cruncher fell asleep. But when he was woken by their return, he went to Mr Lorry and received from him a piece of paper on which had been written the words 'Not Guilty'.

Chapter 4   Sydney Carton

Outside the court Mr Charles Darnay was met by his friends. They were Dr Manette, Lucie Manette, Mr Lorry, Mr Stryver, who had defended him, and Mr Carton, who worked for Mr Stryver.

It would have been difficult to recognize in Dr Manette the shoemaker of Paris. The worst effects of his terrible experience appeared to have left him: his face was cheerful; he stood upright; he looked strong and well. Sometimes, when memories of his time in prison returned to him, a black cloud seemed to settle on him. At such times, only his daughter, Lucie, whom he loved so much, had the power to drive the dark cloud away.

Mr Darnay kissed Miss Manette's hand gratefully, and then warmly thanked Mr Stryver, who said, 'I am glad to have saved your life and honour, Mr Darnay. It was a terrible, false charge against you, but a dangerous one.'

'You saved my life and I shall never forget it,' replied Darnay.

'And now,' said Mr Lorry, 'we have all had a very tiring day. Miss Lucie looks ill; Mr Darnay has had a terrible time, and we are all worn out. Let us all go home and sleep.'

'You speak for yourself,' said Mr Stryver. 'I have a night's work in front of me.'

The Doctor looked at Darnay and a strange expression came over his face as he did so. It was an expression of dislike and even of fear.

'Father,' said Lucie, taking his hand, 'shall we go home?'

A carriage was called and the father and daughter left in it. Mr Stryver also went away, to be followed by Mr Lorry. Only Darnay and Carton were left.

'You look faint, Mr Darnay,' said Carton.

'I feel rather faint,' replied Darnay.

'Then come and drink some wine with me. I know a place where the wine is good.'

Soon the two men were seated opposite each other.

'Do you feel that you belong to the world again?' asked Carton.

'Yes. I am still confused, but I think I do.'

Carton filled a glass with wine and emptied it.

'That must give you satisfaction,' he said. 'As for myself, my great desire is to forget that I belong to it. The world has no good in it for me, and I am of no good to the world.'

Charles Darnay did not know how to answer.

Carton continued, 'Miss Manette is a very beautiful young lady, my friend. What does it feel like to be pitied and cried over by such a fair young woman? She did pity you and cry over you; I saw her myself.'

Again Darnay did not answer, but he thanked him for his help at the trial.

'I neither want your thanks nor deserve them,' replied the other. 'Mr Darnay, let me ask you a question: do you think I like you?'

'Really, Mr Carton, I haven't thought about it.'

'Well, think about it now.'

'You have acted as if you like me,' answered Darnay, 'but I don't think you do.'

'And I don't think I do either.'

'But,' said Darnay, 'there is nothing to prevent our parting in a friendly manner. Let me pay the bill.'

'Certainly,' said Carton. 'Do you wish to pay for both of us?'

'Yes, I do,' answered Darnay.

'Then bring me some more wine, waiter,' said Carton, 'and come and wake me at ten o'clock.'

The bill having been paid, Darnay wished Carton good night. When he was alone, Carton rose and looked at himself in a mirror that hung on the wall. He saw in himself a man who had great powers of mind and a good heart, but these powers had never been properly used. He was angry with Darnay because Darnay was so like him in appearance but so much above him in other ways. And there was Lucie; the thought of Lucie filled his heart with hatred for the other man. He drank more wine, put his head on his arms and fell asleep.

After some hours Carton was woken by the waiter and took himself to Mr Stryver's rooms to help him get his papers ready for the next day's cases.

Sydney Carton did the work while Stryver sat in an armchair and watched him. Both of them made frequent use of a bottle of wine, for those were the days when most men drank heavily. When Carton had prepared the papers, he passed them to Mr Stryver. Then they discussed the cases together and drank some more wine.

'And now we have finished, Sydney,' said Mr Stryver. 'You prepared today's case very well. You were very good. Every question had its effect. You completely defeated those witnesses.'

'I am always good, am I not?' replied Carton.

'I won't disagree with that. But what has made your temper so bad? You are always the same. The same old Sydney Carton who was with me at school. Now in high spirits, now in the depths of misery.'

'Yes, the same person and with the same bad luck. Even when I was at school I did exercises for the other boys instead of doing my own.'

'It was always your own fault. There is never any energy or purpose in your efforts. Why have I been so successful and you so unsuccessful?'

'Partly because you pay me to help you, I suppose. But you were always far in front and I was always far behind.'

'Yes,' said Stryver, 'you have fallen into your right place and I have fallen into mine.'

'Even when we were students together in Paris,' continued Carton, 'you were always somewhere and I was always nowhere.'

'And whose fault was that?'

'Don't let's talk about it.'

'Well, then, let's drink a last glass to the health of the pretty witness,' said Stryver.

'She's not pretty.'

'But she is. She attracted the admiration of the whole court.'

'That court is no judge of beauty.'

'You surprise me. I thought at the time that you were very much attracted to her. You were very quick to see what happened to her.'

'Everybody saw what happened to her. And now I'll have no more to drink. I'll get to bed.'

He left the house and made his way through the cold sad streets. Reaching his own rooms, he threw himself down on the unmade bed whose sheets he had often made wet with wasted tears.

Here was a good man, a clever man; but he had never been able to make anything of himself or to find peace.

Chapter 5   Dr Manette in London

One Sunday afternoon, four months after the trial of Charles Darnay, Mr Jarvis Lorry was walking along the sunny streets. He was on his way to have dinner with his friend, Dr Manette. The Doctor lived on two floors of a building in a quiet London street: there he was able to earn as much as he needed by receiving those who came to ask his medical advice.

On arriving at the house, Mr Lorry rang the doorbell.

'Is Dr Manette at home?'

'Not yet, sir.'

'Is Miss Lucie at home?'

'Not yet, sir.'

'Is Miss Pross at home?'

'I'm not sure, sir.'

'Well, I'll go upstairs and wait.'

The Doctor's daughter had made the house comfortable and attractive, for she had clever hands and good taste. There were three rooms on each floor, and the doors between them were open so that the air might pass freely through them all. As he walked from one to another, Mr Lorry noticed that in the third room, in a corner, stood the disused shoemaker's bench and the tools that the Doctor had once used in the wine shop in Paris.

'I am surprised,' said Mr Lorry aloud, 'that he keeps anything to remind him of his sufferings.'

'And why are you surprised at that?' said the sharp voice of Miss Pross, making Mr Lorry jump. 'How do you do?'

'I am quite well, thank you. And how are you?'

'I am very anxious about my young lady.'

'May I ask the cause?'

'All kinds of unsuitable people keep coming to see her. Too many of them.'

Mr Lorry knew that Miss Pross was angry when other people

paid attention to Lucie. He also knew that she was one of those women who thought nothing of their own needs and who, through pure love and admiration, are ready to make themselves slaves to youth when they have lost it, to beauty which they have never had, and to bright hopes that have never shone upon their own dark lives. He knew that there was nothing better in the world than the honest service of the heart, and he respected Miss Pross far more than many rich ladies who had money in Tellson's Bank.

'Let me ask you a question,' he said. 'Does the Doctor, in talking to Lucie, never mention the shoemaking time?'

'Never.'

'Is that not rather strange? We all know that he is not guilty of any crime. Why should he never mention it?'

'I think he is afraid of losing his memory again. That would make the subject unpleasant to him.'

'True.'

'Sometimes he gets up in the middle of the night,' went on Miss Pross, 'and walks up and down, up and down, in his room. Then my young lady goes to him, and they walk up and down together until he is less troubled. But he never says a word of the cause of his restlessness to her.'

Just then they heard the sound of footsteps in the street, as though the mention of the endless walking up and down had caused it.

'Here they are!' said Miss Pross.

Miss Pross was a pleasant sight as she took off Lucie's coat and hat and smoothed her rich hair. Lucie was a pleasant sight, too, as she thanked her; and the Doctor smiled as he said that Miss Pross spoilt his daughter by being too kind to her.

After dinner they went out and sat in the garden. While they were there, Mr Darnay arrived to see them and was kindly received by Dr Manette and Lucie, though Miss Pross looked rather angry and left them.

As they sat and talked, the conversation turned to the subject of the old buildings of London.

'Have you seen much of the Tower of London?' said Mr Darnay to the Doctor, in the course of this conversation.

'Lucie and I have been there. We have seen enough of it to know that it is very interesting.'

'I have been there, as you know,' said Darnay, a little angrily. 'I was there when I was being tried as an enemy of the King; so I was not able to see much of it. They told me something strange when I was there.'

'What was that?' Lucie asked.

'While doing some repairs, some workmen had found an old, forgotten room. The walls were covered with dates, names, prayers and such things written by the old prisoners. One of the words written there was DIG. As a result, the floor below was examined carefully; and there, under a stone, were found the ashes of some paper and the remains of a leather bag. What the unknown prisoner had written will never be read, but he had written something.'

'Father!' cried Lucie. 'Are you ill?'

Dr Manette had suddenly jumped up with his hand to his head. His look frightened them all.

'No, my dear, not ill. There are large drops of rain falling and they made me jump. We had better go in.'

He seemed better almost immediately. Rain was really falling and he showed the back of his hand with drops on it. Mr Lorry thought he saw on the Doctor's face, when his eyes rested on Darnay, the same strange look that had been on it when he saw him outside the court.

At teatime, Mr Carton called. He stood leaning against the window, while the others sat near it watching the rain falling outside.

21

'A storm is coming,' said Dr Manette. 'But it is coming slowly.'

'It is coming surely,' said Carton.

It came at last. The rush and roar of the rain and the storm of thunder and lightning were so severe that no voice could be heard. It lasted until after the moon rose at midnight.

As the guests left, the great bell of St Paul's struck one in the cleared air.

'Good night, Mr Carton,' said Mr Lorry. 'Good night, Mr Darnay. Shall we ever see such a night again together?'

Chapter 6   The Accident in Paris

The Marquis of Evrémonde left the Minister's house. He went down the great stairway into the courtyard, got into his carriage and was driven away. He was in a very bad temper. The Minister had behaved coldly to him and hardly anyone had spoken to him.

Because of this, it was rather pleasant for him to see the common people scatter from in front of his horses, often only just escaping being run over. His servant drove as if he were charging an enemy, and his master made no attempt to control him. There had been some complaints that the careless driving of the rich through these narrow streets made it dangerous for the common people. But nothing had been done, and the poor were left to save themselves if they could.

The carriage charged through the streets and round the corners with women running out and dragging little children out of the way. At a narrow street corner, one of the wheels passed over a small child. There was a loud cry from a number of voices, the horses were pulled up, and the carriage came to a stop.

'What is wrong?' asked the Marquis calmly, looking out of the window.

A tall man had run to the little body and was holding it in his arms and crying aloud.

'Pardon, Monsieur the Marquis,' said one of the men in the street. 'It is a child.'

'But why is he making such a terrible noise? Is it his own child?'

'Excuse me, Monsieur the Marquis. It is.'

The tall man got up suddenly from the ground and came running towards the carriage. The Marquis put his hand to his sword.

'Killed!' cried the man, raising his arms above his head. 'Dead!'

The people closed round and looked at the Marquis. They said nothing, but watched him with hatred in their eyes.

The Marquis looked at them all as if they were rats that had come out of their holes. He took out a bag of money.

'It is unbelievable to me,' said he, 'that you people cannot take care of yourselves and your children. You are always getting in the way. How do I know that you have not harmed the horses? See, give him that.'

He threw out a gold coin and all eyes looked at it as it fell to the ground. The tall man cried again, 'Dead!'

The crowd parted and made way for another man. On seeing him, the tall man fell on his shoulders, crying, and pointed to some women who were bending over the little body. But they were silent, as were the men.

'I saw it happen. I know everything,' said the latecomer. 'Be brave, my Gaspard. It is perhaps better for the poor little child to die in this way than to live. He died in a moment, without pain. Could he have lived without pain?'

'You, there!' called the Marquis. 'You are a wise man. What do they call you?'

'They call me Defarge.'

'Of what trade?'

'A wine seller.'

'Pick that up, wise man and wine seller,' said the Marquis, throwing out another gold coin, 'and spend it as you wish. The horses there, are they unhurt?'

Without troubling to look at the people again, Monsieur leaned back in his seat and was about to drive away. He had the air of a gentleman who had accidentally broken some common thing and had paid for it. But he was suddenly interrupted by a gold coin flying into the carriage and ringing on the floor.

'Stop,' said the Marquis. 'Hold the horses. Who threw that?'

He looked at the spot where Defarge had stood, but he was no longer there. In his place there stood the figure of a large dark woman, knitting.

'You dogs,' said the Marquis, calmly and without raising his voice. 'I would ride over any one of you. If I knew which one of you threw that, I would crush him under my carriage wheels.'

They were like slaves – so frightened of the aristocracy that not one of the men dared look him in the eyes. But the woman who stood there knitting looked at him: she looked him steadily in the face. He pretended not to notice her, leaned back in his seat again and gave the word, 'Go on.'

He was driven quickly away, away through the miserable streets of Paris and out into the open country. The carriage rolled through beautiful countryside, but the crops in the fields were poor, as poor as the workers who tried to make them grow. Even the land seemed to share the misery of the people.

Towards sunset, the carriage was pulled slowly up a steep hill. A roadmender looked at it as it passed him, looked with surprise in his eyes, then ran ahead of it to the top of the hill and looked hard at it again as it passed. Then it rolled quickly down the hill into a village. All the villagers were poor, and many of them were sitting at their doors preparing for supper what little they had been able to find. Few children could be seen, and no dogs. Heavy taxes had almost killed the village – the tax for the state, the tax for the church, the tax for the land, the local tax and the general tax – it was surprising that any people remained in the village at all.

The carriage stopped in the village. The people looked silently at it and the Marquis looked at the people. The roadmender came down the hill.

'Bring that man here,' said the Marquis to his driver.

The man was brought.

'I passed you on the road.'

'Yes. Monsieur. I had the honour to be passed by you.'

'I passed you on the hill and then again at the top. Why were you looking at the carriage so strangely?'

'Monsieur, I was looking at the man. There was a man under the carriage. He was hanging on by the chain.'

'Who was he? You know all the men in these parts. Who was he?'

'Pardon, Monsieur. He was not from this area. He was a stranger. I never saw him before.'

'What was he like?'

'Monsieur, he was all covered with dust, as white as a ghost, as tall as a ghost.'

'What happened to him? Did he run away?'

'Monsieur, he ran away down the hill as if the devil was after him.'

'You are crazy!' said Monsieur. 'He was probably a thief and you said nothing. Go away. Monsieur Gabelle!'

Gabelle worked for the Marquis. He collected the taxes and the rents for him.

'If this man comes to the village, arrest him, Gabelle.'

'Monsieur, I shall be happy to carry out your orders.'

'Go on,' said the Marquis.

It was quite dark when the Marquis came to the castle where he lived. Servants with lights in their hands came out to meet him. The great door was opened for him.

'I expect young Charles from London. Has he arrived yet?'

'Not yet, Monsieur.'

Chapter 7   Darnay and his Uncle the Marquis

The Marquis went up the broad steps of his home. A light was carried before him. He crossed the great hall and went upstairs to his three private rooms, in the third of which a supper table was laid for two.

'Charles has not arrived, I hear,' he said. 'I do not suppose he will come tonight now, but leave the table as it is. I shall be ready in a quarter of an hour.'

As he was eating his supper, he heard the sound of wheels; he sent orders that Charles was to be told that supper was ready for him. In a short time he came: he had been known in England as Charles Darnay.

'You left Paris yesterday, sir?' he said to the Marquis, as he took his seat at the table.

'Yesterday. And you?'

'I came direct from London.'

'You have been away a long time.'

'I have been kept by various business matters.'

'No doubt,' said the uncle.

'I fell into great danger when I was there. I wonder if you were responsible for the situation I found myself in.'

'No, no, no,' said the uncle pleasantly.

Charles looked at the Marquis with deep distrust. 'I know that you would stop me if you could. I am very glad that you are not well liked at Court, for if you had more influence there, you would have me put in prison.'

'It is possible,' said the Marquis with great calmness. 'For the honour of the family, I would even do that.'

'I see that, happily for me, you were again received coldly.'

'I am sorry to say,' replied the uncle, 'that the King does not help the aristocracy as much as he did. It used not to be so, but in all such things France has changed for the worse. Our fathers had the power of life and death over the surrounding people, but we have lost many rights. All very bad, very bad.'

'We have behaved ourselves so badly, both in the past and in the present,' said Charles sadly, 'that I believe our name to be more hated than any name in France.'

'Let us hope so. It shows respect.'

'The only respect I see around us is the respect of fear and slavery. I hate the system that my father, your brother, left me. I am part of it, but powerless in it, trying to follow my dying mother's last request that I should show kindness, and repair the wrongs that have been done.'

'Do not ask for my help because I will never give it.'

'This property and France are lost to me,' said Charles. 'I give them up.'

'It is not yet your property.'

'If it passed to me tomorrow, I would not accept it.'

'I hope and believe that that is not likely.'

'It is built on misery and ruin. It is a tower of waste, mismanagement, debt, hunger and suffering!'

'Ha!' said the Marquis in a well-satisfied manner.

'If it ever becomes mine, I shall give it to someone who can free it from the weight that drags it down.'

'And you?' said the uncle. 'How do you intend to live?'

'I shall work.'

'In England, I suppose?'

'Yes. The family name cannot suffer from me there, since I do not bear it there.'

'You know a Frenchman who has found safety there?' asked the Marquis.

'Yes.'

'A doctor with a daughter?'

'Yes.'

'Yes,' said the Marquis. 'You are tired. Good night.'

As he bent his head politely, there was a secrecy in his expression which struck Charles powerfully; but he knew that it would be useless to ask any questions.

'Good night!' said the uncle. 'Sleep well! Light Monsieur to his room . . . and burn him in his bed if you like,' he added softly to himself.

After Charles had gone, the Marquis himself went to his room. Darkness fell on the great building, as it had fallen on the country around it. The hungry dreamed of good food, and the tired of rest. Then came the beginnings of the new day as the sun poured its light on castle and tree, on field and village. Men and women came out into the cold morning to their work, some to dig in the fields, some to lead their thin cows to any grass that might be found by the roadside.

The castle awoke later: windows were thrown open; horses looked over their shoulders at the light and freshness pouring in at the doorways; dogs pulled hard at their chains, impatient to be let loose. All these were the usual events of the return of morning. But why did the great bell of the castle ring? Why did men run up and down the stairs? Why did others hurry to prepare their horses and ride away into the distance? What was the meaning of all this excitement?

The meaning was to be found in the bed of the Marquis.

Driven into the heart of the still figure which lay in that bed was a knife; and round the handle of the knife was a piece of paper bearing in rough writing the words:

'Drive him fast to his grave. This is from JACQUES.'

Chapter 8   Darnay Speaks of Love

Twelve months had passed and Mr Charles Darnay was firmly settled in England as a teacher of French language and literature. Some of his time he spent at Cambridge, where he became known as an excellent teacher for those students who studied modern languages. The rest of his time he was in London.

It was a year since he had left France; the memory of the castle and his murdered uncle was like a bad dream. He was young, and in love. He had loved Lucie Manette from the hour of his danger. He had never heard a sound so sweet as the sound of her gentle voice, never seen a face so sweet as the face he saw opposite him when he stood on the edge of the grave. But he had not spoken to her on the subject. He had never spoken of his love to anyone.

Now it was a summer day. He had recently arrived back from Cambridge and had decided to speak to Dr Manette about his love for Lucie. He was on his way to the Doctor's house and he knew that Lucie was out with Miss Pross.

He found the Doctor in his armchair at a window. The energy that had supported him in his terrible sufferings had largely returned to him. Now he was strong both in mind and body. He studied a lot and had begun his medical work again. He was usually very cheerful; and only very, very rarely did a black cloud overshadow the brightness of his mind. When Darnay entered, he laid down his book and held out his hand.

'Charles Darnay! I am so pleased to see you,' said Dr Manette.

'We have been expecting you for several days. Mr Stryver and Mr Carton were here yesterday; they were both saying that you were later than usual.'

Darnay was not very pleased to hear that these two had been in the house. He inquired about Miss Manette's health.

'She is well. She has gone out with Miss Pross, but she will soon be back.'

'Dr Manette, I knew that she was away. I have taken the opportunity of her being away from home to beg to speak to you.'

There was a pause.

'Yes?' said the Doctor doubtfully. 'Bring up your chair and speak on.'

'I have had the happiness during the last 18 months of being a frequent visitor in your house. I hope that the subject on which I am about to speak will –'

'Is Lucie the subject?'

'She is. Dear Dr Manette, I love your daughter fondly, deeply, dearly. If there was ever love in the world, I love her. You have loved yourself; let your old love speak for me.'

The Doctor sat with his face turned away. Darnay's words had brought a look of deep pain into his eyes.

'Not that, sir! Don't speak of that, I beg you.'

His cry was like a cry of actual pain. He held out his hand as if to beg Darnay to be silent. Darnay said nothing for a time.

'I ask your pardon,' said the Doctor in a low voice. 'I do not doubt your love for Lucie. Have you spoken to her?'

'No, sir, nor have I written to her. And you know why. I know how much your daughter means to you. I know that since you returned to life, she has been more to you than a daughter or a wife. I know that her love for you and your love for her are the greatest things in both your lives.'

Dr Manette sat silently with his face bent down. He breathed

30

rather quickly, but he showed no other sign of his deep feelings.

'Dear Dr Manette, seeing how much you mean to each other, I have controlled myself as long as I could. But I love her; Heaven is my witness that I love her.'

'I believe it,' answered the father sadly.

'Do not fear that if ever I am lucky enough to win Lucie for my wife, there will be any question of my putting any separation between you and her. That is not my intention now: nor will it ever be.'

He put his hand on the Doctor's arm. 'No, sir. Like you, I have been driven from France by misgovernment and misery. Like you, I am earning my own living in a foreign land. I desire only to share your fortunes, share your life and hopes, and to be true to you until death. I do not desire to come between you and Lucie, but to add my love to that which unites you both.'

The father looked up. A struggle was going on in his mind. There was something in Darnay's face that brought back to him bitter memories, memories that he tried to shut out of his thoughts.

'You speak manfully, Charles Darnay, and I thank you. I will speak freely with you. Have you any reason to believe that Lucie returns your love?'

'None, yet, none.'

'Do you desire my permission to speak to her?'

'No, sir, not yet.'

'Then what do you want from me?'

'I want a promise that if Lucie ever tells you that she loves me, you will not say anything against me, but that you will tell her what I have said. I know that she would never accept me if she thought that it would make any difference to your happiness.'

'I promise,' said the Doctor. 'If at any time she tells me that you are necessary to her happiness, I will give her to you.

31

Nothing shall prevent it, not even the memory of my lost years and my great wrongs.'

'Thank you. Your confidence in me ought to be returned with full confidence on my part. My present name, though only slightly changed from my mother's, is not, as I have previously told you, my real name. I wish to tell you what my real name is, and why I am in England.'

'Stop!' said the Doctor.

'I wish to tell you so that I may deserve your confidence and have no secret from you.'

'Stop! I do not wish to hear. Tell me when I ask you, not now. If you should be successful, if Lucie should love you, you may tell me on your marriage morning. Do you promise?'

'I promise.'

'Give me your hand. She will be home soon. It is better that she should not see us together tonight. Go! God keep you!'

It was dark when Darnay left him. Some time later Lucie came home. She hurried into the room alone, as Miss Pross had gone upstairs, and was surprised to find the armchair empty.

'Father,' she cried. 'Where are you?'

Nothing was said in reply, but she heard a low hammering coming from his bedroom. She went towards it quietly and looked in, then came away frightened, crying to herself in great terror, 'What shall I do? What shall I do?'

Her uncertainty lasted only for a minute. She walked back to his room, knocked gently on his door and called softly to him. The hammering stopped at the sound of her voice. Soon he came out to her, and they walked up and down together for a long time, she speaking calmly and comfortingly to him.

During the night she got up silently and looked at him in his sleep. He was sleeping deeply; all his shoemaking tools and his old unfinished work were as usual. She returned thankfully to her room.

Chapter 9   Carton Does the Same

'Sydney,' said Mr Stryver on the same night or morning, 'mix me another drink: I have something to say to you.'

For several nights Sydney had been hard at work clearing up Stryver's papers; the courts were closed and there would be no more cases until November. The work was done at last, but it had left him tired out.

'Now, look here!' said Stryver. 'I am going to tell you something that will surprise you. I am going to marry!'

'Good heavens! Do I know her?'

'Guess!'

'I am not going to guess at five o'clock in the morning. My brain won't stand it.'

'Well, then, I'll tell you, if I can make you understand. You know, I am a gentler sort of man than you. I am a man who makes himself more – more –'

'Say more pleasant,' suggested Carton.

'Well, I'll say more pleasant. More pleasant in the presence of women. You've been at Dr Manette's house as much as I have, and I've been ashamed of your bad manners. You are an unpleasant person, Sydney!'

Sydney had a drink and laughed.

'Look at me,' said Stryver. 'Being a successful man, I have less need to make myself pleasant than you have. Why do I do it? I do it because it's wise. I get on in the world!'

'Well, who is the lady?'

'The young lady is Miss Manette. Do you approve?'

'Why should I not approve?' said Sydney.

'You take it more easily than I thought you would. Yes, Sydney, I have had enough of this kind of life with no other as a change from it; I feel that it is a pleasant thing for a man to have a home when he feels ready to go to it. When he doesn't, he can stay away. And I think Miss Manette would suit me. She is an attractive creature and I have made up my mind to please myself. She will have in me a man fairly rich now, and a rapidly rising man. Why don't you get married yourself? You'll be ill some day. You may need someone to look after you.'

'I'll think about it,' said Sydney.

As Mr Stryver had decided to get married, he thought it would be a good thing to start his holiday by going to Miss Manette's to speak his mind. His way led him past Tellson's and, as he knew that Mr Lorry was a friend of the Manettes, he went into the bank to tell him of his bright future.

'Hello!' said Stryver loudly. 'How do you do?'

'What can I do for you?' asked Mr Lorry in a quiet voice, hoping that his caller would speak in the same way.

'Oh! It is a private matter,' said Stryver. 'I am going to offer myself in marriage to your lovely friend, Miss Manette.'

'Oh! Dear me,' cried Mr Lorry, rubbing his nose and looking at his visitor doubtfully.

'Oh! Dear me, sir!' repeated Stryver. 'What do you mean?'

'My meaning is friendly, of course. But, really, you know, Mr Stryver . . .' Mr Lorry paused and shook his head.

'What do you mean, sir? Am I not suitable? Am I not rich? Am I not getting on in the world?'

'Oh! Nobody can doubt that!'

'Then what on earth is your meaning?'

'Well! I . . . Are you going there now?'

'Immediately,' said Stryver, striking the desk.

'Then I think I wouldn't, if I were you.'

'Why? State your reason.'

'I wouldn't go without having some cause to believe that I would succeed.'

'I have just given you three good reasons for success,' said Stryver very angrily.

'When I say succeed, I mean succeed with the young lady.'

'Then you advise me not to go?' said Stryver with an angry laugh.

'I was about to say that you might find it painful if you were mistaken about her feelings; and that Dr Manette might also find it painful to tell you the truth; and that Miss Manette might also find the matter painful. Don't you think it would be better if I tried to find out how she would feel about it, before you go?'

'Very well!' said Stryver. 'Let me know soon. Good morning.' He burst out of the bank, deciding that he must find a way out of this without seeming to mind.

When Mr Lorry called on him that evening, Stryver seemed to have forgotten the matter.

'I have been to the house,' said Mr Lorry, 'and I have no doubt that I was right in our conversation this morning. I do not think that you would succeed with Miss Manette.'

'I am sorry for them,' said Stryver. 'Let us forget the whole thing. If they have no sense, I am well out of it. Young women have been stupid before. There is no harm done. I never asked the young lady to marry me, and to tell you the truth I am not sure that I ever would have done so. Thank you very much for your trouble.'

Mr Lorry was so surprised at these words that he found himself outside before he could collect his thoughts, and as he made his way home he asked himself what in the world Mr Stryver's feelings really were.

When Stryver next met Sydney Carton, he told him that he had thought better of that marrying business, and soon afterwards he went down to Devonshire for a holiday.

But Sydney remained in London, and one day went to call on Lucie Manette. She had never felt quite comfortable with him. On looking at his face, she said, 'I fear you are not well, Mr Carton!'

'No; but the life I lead is not the kind to make me healthy.'

'Forgive me for mentioning it, but is it not a pity to live no better life?'

Looking at him again, she was surprised and saddened to see that there were tears in his eyes. There were tears in his voice, too, as he answered:

'It is too late for that. I shall never be better than I am. I shall sink lower and lower.' He covered his face with his hands.

She had never seen him like this before, and felt very sorry for him.

'Please forgive me, Miss Manette. I am troubled by the knowledge of what I want to say to you. Will you hear me?'

'If it would make you happier, Mr Carton, it would make me glad.'

'God keep you, Miss Manette. Don't be afraid to hear me. I am like one who died young. All my life might have been better, but it is too late now.'

'No, Mr Carton! I am sure that the future might still hold the best part of it!' She was pale and shaking as she spoke.

'Even if it were possible, Miss Manette, for you to return my love, I should only bring you to misery and pull you down with me. But I know very well that you can have no romantic feelings for me; I ask for none; I am even thankful that it cannot be.'

'Without it, can I not save you, Mr Carton?'

'No. If you will listen to me a little longer, all that you can ever do for me will be done. I wish you to know that you have been the last dream of my soul. The sight of you with your father, and of this home made by you, has stirred old feelings that I thought had died out of me. Since I met you, I have begun to feel bad about my terrible life. I have thought of trying to start again. All a dream! But I wish you to know that you caused it.'

'Will nothing of it remain? Oh, Mr Carton, try again!'

'No, it is useless. Only let me carry, through the rest of my miserable life, the memory that I opened my heart to you. Will you let me believe, when I remember this day, that my secret lies safely in your heart, and will be shared by no one?'

'If that will give you comfort, yes.'

'Thank you. And again, God keep you!'

He put her hand to his lips and moved towards the door.

'I shall never mention this subject again,' he said. 'When I die, I shall remember that you were the last person to whom I opened my heart.'

He was so unlike himself, and it was so sad to think how much he had thrown away, that Lucie Manette cried as he stood looking back at her.

'Do not cry. I am not worth such feeling. In an hour or two, I shall be with my low friends again. I have one last request and then I will go. It is useless to say it, I know, but it rises out of my soul. It is this. For you, and for anyone dear to you, I would do anything. I would accept any difficulty to help you and those you love. Always remember, in the happy days to come, that there is a man who would give his life to keep a life you loved beside you.'

He said 'Goodbye'; and with a last 'God keep you,' he left her.

Chapter 10   The Roadmender

The people of Saint-Antoine had been waiting for several days for news of what had happened to one of their friends, Gaspard. He had been seized by the police and taken to the village where he had killed the Marquis. They were expecting Monsieur Defarge to bring them the news. Many of them waited long hours in the wine shop where Madame Defarge sat, calm and silent, knitting.

At last, at about midday, two dusty figures passed through the streets: one was the owner of the wine shop and the other a roadmender in a blue cap. Many eyes noticed them, but no one followed them as they passed, and no one spoke as they entered the wine shop, though the eyes of everyone were turned on them.

'Good day, gentlemen,' said Monsieur Defarge.

Immediately every tongue was loosened and there came an answering cry of 'Good day'.

'It is bad weather, gentlemen,' said Defarge, shaking his head. When they heard these words, every man looked at his neighbour and then all looked down and were silent. One man got up and went out.

'Wife,' said Defarge, addressing Madame Defarge, 'I have travelled a long way with this fine mender of roads. He is a good man and is called Jacques. Give him something to drink.'

A second man got up and went out. Madame Defarge set wine in front of the mender of roads called Jacques; he took off his cap to the company and drank. A third man got up and went out.

Monsieur Defarge, too, refreshed himself with some wine. He looked at no one present, and no one looked at him, not even Madame Defarge, who had again taken up her knitting.

'Have you finished, my friend?' he asked at length.

'Yes, thank you.'

'Come along then. You shall see the room that is ready for you. It will suit you excellently.'

They went out of the shop and into the courtyard, then up steep stairs into a narrow room, the same room where once a white-haired man had sat making shoes.

There was no white-haired man there now; but three men were there, the same three who had once looked through a hole in the door at the old man, the same three men who had gone out of the wine shop one by one – the three Jacques.

Defarge closed the door carefully and spoke in a low voice:

'Jacques One, Jacques Two, Jacques Three, this is the witness that I, Jacques Four, met as ordered. He will tell you all. Speak, Jacques Five.'

The roadmender looked at them.

'Where shall I begin, Monsieur?'

'Begin right at the beginning.'

'I saw Gaspard first about a year ago, under the carriage of the Marquis, hanging on by the chain. The carriage was going up a steep hill.'

Jacques Three asked how he had afterwards recognized him.

'By his tall figure. When the Marquis asked me what he was like, I answered "Tall as a ghost!" '

'You should have said that he was short,' said Jacques Two.

'But at that time he had not done anything. Well, he ran away. The Marquis was murdered. He disappeared. They searched for him high and low. How many months – ten, eleven?'

'Never mind how many,' said Defarge. 'Unluckily he was caught in the end. Go on.'

'Once again I was at work on the hillside. I saw six soldiers coming. In the middle of them was a tall man with his arms tied to his sides. They were all covered with dust, and as they passed I recognized the tall man. But this time he could not run away down the hillside. "Come on" said the leader of the soldiers. "Bring him quickly to his grave." Then they pushed him down the hill into the village. He fell, they picked him up again and laughed when they saw his face all covered with blood. They brought him into the village, and all the villagers came out to see. Through its streets they went, straight up to the prison. The prison gates opened and swallowed him – like this.'

He opened his mouth as wide as he could and then closed it suddenly.

'Go on, Jacques Five,' said Defarge.

'All the villagers whispered in the streets. The whole village went to sleep, and in their sleep they dreamed of the unhappy man up there, who would never come down again except to his death. In the morning he could be seen high up in a little room, looking out from behind iron bars, looking out at the countryside where he would never walk again.'

The four listeners looked darkly at one another. Anger was clear on every face. Yet they had the appearance of being judges in a law court as they listened to the roadmender.

'For seven days he remained up there,' said the roadmender. 'All the village looked up at him, but secretly, because they were afraid. During the evening, when the villagers got together in the square, all faces were turned towards the prison. Some of them said that he would not be put to death, that a letter had been sent to the King explaining that he was made crazy by the death of his child.'

'Listen, you,' said Jacques One. 'A letter was sent to the King. All here except yourself saw the King take it, in his carriage, in the street, sitting beside the Queen. It was Defarge here, who, at the risk of his own life, ran out in front of the horses with the letter in his hand.'

'And know, too,' said Jacques Three, 'that the King's guards surrounded him and struck him.'

'Go on,' said Defarge.

'On Monday morning, when the village woke, there was a gallows 40 feet high in the middle of the square.'

He pointed with his finger as if to show the height of the gallows.

'All work was stopped in the village: nobody took the cows out; everybody went to the square. At midday there was a sound of drums, and down from the prison he came, surrounded by a group of soldiers. He was tied up as before, and in his mouth was a cloth to prevent him from speaking. And so, without speaking, he was hanged there, 40 feet high, and was left there, hanging in the square. It was frightful. How could the women go near that place? How could the children play there with that thing above them throwing down its shadow?

'It was terrible. I left the village on Monday evening, and as I left it I looked back and saw the long shadow of the gallows lying across the church, across the houses and even across the prison. I met this gentleman as I had been warned I should. With him, I came on, first walking, then riding, all yesterday and all last night. And here you see me.'

After a long silence, the first Jacques said, 'Good, you have acted and spoken truthfully. Will you wait for us a little, outside the door?'

'Of course,' said the mender of roads. Defarge got up and went with him to the top of the stairs, and then returned.

'What do you say, Jacques?' said Number One. 'Shall we put them on the list?'

'On the list for destruction – yes,' said Defarge.

'The castle and all the family of Evrémonde?' inquired the first.

'The castle and all the family,' replied Defarge.

'Are you sure,' said Number One, 'that the list is quite safe? It is true that it is written in secret writing, and nobody but ourselves can read it. But what if we are caught? Can your wife read it when the time comes?'

'Jacques,' replied Defarge with confidence, 'do not be afraid. The list is not necessary to my wife. When a name is listed, that name is written in the memory of my wife. She repeats the name to herself as she knits, and she knits every name into her memory. Not a letter of a name will ever be lost from the knitted list of Madame Defarge.'

They all showed their approval, and one asked, 'What about

the roadmender? Is he to be sent back soon? He is very simple. Is he not a little dangerous?'

'He knows nothing,' said Defarge. 'I will look after him. He wishes to see the fine world, the King, the Queen and the Court. He'll see them on Sunday and then I'll send him back.'

'What! Is it wise to let him see the King and the aristocracy?'

'Jacques,' said Defarge, 'if you show a cat milk, it will want to drink it. If you show a dog a rabbit, it will hunt and kill it some day.'

Nothing more was said, and the men went their separate ways.

For several days the roadmender stayed in the wine shop. His life was new and pleasant, but Madame Defarge frightened him; she was always silent, always knitting, and she took no notice of his presence; he shook in his wooden shoes whenever he looked at her. He was not at all pleased on Sunday to learn that she was to go with him and Defarge to Versailles to see the King.

As usual Madame Defarge took her knitting with her, and went on with it even in the public carriage that carried them there.

'You work hard, Madame,' said one of the passengers.

'Yes,' said Madame, 'I have a great deal to do.'

'What are you making, Madame?'

'Many things.'

'For example?'

'For example,' said Madame Defarge, 'clothes for the grave.'

The man moved away from her as soon as he could. The roadmender, too, was troubled by her words, but he forgot everything when he saw the King and his fair-haired Queen in their golden carriage, attended by all the lords and ladies of the Court. Such a crowd of laughing ladies and fine lords, such jewels, such bright silk, such proud faces! The roadmender forgot everything, took off his cap, waved it and shouted, 'Long live the

King! Long live the Queen!' as loudly as anyone.

'Ha!' said Defarge when all was over. 'You are a good man.'

The roadmender now began to ask himself if he had not made himself look stupid; but no.

'You are just the man we want,' said Defarge in his ear. 'You make these aristocrats think that it will last for ever. So our job will be easier.'

The roadmender agreed.

Defarge went on. 'These lords and ladies know nothing. They treat you badly and think far more of their horses and dogs than of you. So let us deceive them a little longer. Our day will come.'

Madame Defarge looked coldly at the roadmender and said, 'Listen, you. If you were shown some pretty birds that could not fly, and were told to tear off their feathers for yourself, you would start by tearing off the finest feathers, would you not?'

'That's true, Madame, yes.'

'You have seen fine birds today,' said Madame Defarge, waving her hand in the direction the great ones had gone. 'Now, go home.'

Chapter 11   The Spy

As the Defarges were making their way through the black mud of the streets on their return, Madame said to her husband, 'What did Jacques of the police tell you?'

'Very little tonight. But he said that there is a new spy coming to our part of the city.'

'Oh, well! It is necessary to put him on the list. What is his name?'

'John Barsad. He is English.'

'Good. Is anything known of his appearance?'

'"Age about forty years; average height, black hair; face thin

43

and long; nose bent to the left." '

'Very clear,' said Madame. 'He shall be put on the list.' They reached the shop at midnight and Madame Defarge counted the money that had been taken during their absence, while her husband walked up and down smoking his pipe. Although she was busy with the accounts, she noticed that he seemed a little tired and sad.

'You are faint of heart tonight,' said she.

'A little,' he replied. 'It is a long time.'

'Yes, it is a long time,' she said calmly. 'But revenge takes a long time to prepare. We must wait patiently. Remember that each day that passes brings it nearer. Look around at the evil and injustices of the world. Do you think they can last?'

'You are right. But it is possible that the end may not come in our lifetimes.'

'Even if that is true, we shall have helped it to come. Whatever we can do will help. I myself believe that we shall live to see the victory.'

At midday the next day Madame was knitting in her usual place when a stranger entered the shop. She pinned a rose in her hair as she noticed him, and most of the talking stopped. Gradually people began to leave the shop.

'Good day, Madame,' said the stranger.

'Good day, Monsieur,' she said out loud, but to herself she added, 'Ha! Age about forty; height about five feet nine; black hair; face long and thin; nose bent to the left! Good day!'

'You knit with great skill, Madame!' said the newcomer after ordering some wine.

'I have been doing it for many years.'

'What is it for?'

'To pass the time.'

'Is business good?'

'Business is very bad. The people are so poor.'

'Ah, the unfortunate people. So badly treated, as you say.'

'As you say,' corrected Madame.

'Pardon me. It was I who said so, but of course you think so.'

'I think?' replied Madame in a high voice. 'I and my husband have enough to do keeping this wine shop open, without thinking. All we think about is how to live.'

The spy, who was there to pick up any information he could find or make, did not let his disappointment show in his face, but continued:

'A bad business, this, about poor Gaspard!'

'If people use knives for such purposes,' said Madame calmly, 'they have to pay for it.'

'I believe,' said the spy, lowering his voice, 'that there is a lot of support for the poor man in this neighbourhood, and much anger at his death.'

'Is there? Ah! Here is my husband!'

'Good day, Jacques!' said the spy, touching his hat.

Defarge stopped suddenly and looked hard at him.

'Good day, Jacques!' repeated the spy.

'You are mistaken,' said the keeper of the wine shop. 'That is not my name. I am Ernest Defarge.'

'It is all the same,' said the spy, disappointed again. 'Good day!'

'Good day!' answered Defarge calmly.

'I was just saying to Madame that there was a lot of support and anger in Saint-Antoine for poor Gaspard.'

'No one has told me so. I know nothing of it.'

The spy drank up his wine and asked for more.

'Your name, Monsieur Defarge, makes me think of your old master, Dr Manette. When he was set free, I believe he came to you.'

'That is true.'

'I have known Dr Manette and his daughter in England. Do

you hear much of them now?'

'No.'

'She is going to be married. But not to an Englishman. Remembering Gaspard, poor Gaspard, it is strange that she is going to be married to a relative of the Marquis that Gaspard killed. Her future husband is, of course, the present Marquis. But he lives unknown in England. He is no Marquis there. He is Mr Charles Darnay. D'Aulnais is the name of his mother's family, and he has spelt the name in an English way.'

This piece of news did not seem to affect Madame Defarge in any way, but it affected her husband. Although he tried to appear perfectly calm, he was unable to prevent his hand from shaking as he lit his pipe. The spy would have been no spy if he had failed to notice it.

Having had, at least, one little success, Barsad paid for his drink and left. For some minutes afterwards husband and wife remained exactly as he had left them, fearing that he might come back.

'Can it be true?' said Defarge in a low voice.

'As he has said it,' replied Madame, 'it is probably false. But it may be true.'

'If it is, and if the end comes while we live, I hope her husband stays out of France.'

'He will go where he is to go and will die as he is to die. That is all I know.'

In the evening Madame Defarge used to pass from place to place in Saint-Antoine, visiting the women who knitted like herself. They knitted useless things, but the endless work served them in place of eating and drinking; the hands moved instead of the mouth. If the thin fingers had been still, the stomachs would have noticed their hunger more.

As the darkness fell, another darkness was closing in on France. The church bells, then ringing pleasantly in the evening air, would be melted into guns, and a voice which that night was all powerful would be silenced in death. And the women who knitted in Saint-Antoine would soon be knitting near a thing still unbuilt and counting the heads that dropped from it – they would be knitting near the guillotine.

Chapter 12   Joy and Sorrow

It was the day of Lucie Manette's marriage to Charles Darnay. The morning sun was shining brightly. Mr Lorry, Lucie and Miss Pross were outside the Doctor's door. Inside, the Doctor and Charles were talking. Soon they would all go to the church.

Lucie looked very beautiful. Neither Mr Lorry nor Miss Pross could admire her too much.

'And so, my dear,' said Mr Lorry, 'it was for this that I brought you safely across from France, a baby in my arms, so many years ago. Mr Charles ought to be grateful to me, don't you think so, Miss Pross?'

'Nonsense,' said Miss Pross. 'You didn't do it for him, so he has nothing to be grateful to you for.'

'Perhaps you are right,' said Mr Lorry. 'But why are you crying?'

Miss Pross was so happy that there were tears in her eyes. But she had one secret sorrow. It was that her brother Solomon (who had robbed her and left her many years ago, but whom she still loved) was not to be dear Lucie's husband.

'I'm not crying,' said Miss Pross. 'But I can see tears in your eyes.'

'In my eyes? Nonsense,' said Mr Lorry. 'And now, my dear Lucie, let me give you a kiss and my best wishes before Charles comes out and claims you for his own.'

The door of the Doctor's room opened and he came out with

Charles Darnay. His face was deathly pale, but his manner was calm and he appeared cheerful. The keen eye of Mr Lorry was not deceived; he knew that something had happened inside the room that had given him a great shock.

The Doctor gave his arm to his daughter and took her downstairs to the carriage that Mr Lorry had hired for the occasion. The others followed in another carriage, and soon, in a neighbouring church, with no strangers present, Lucie Manette and Charles Darnay became man and wife.

They returned to the house for breakfast, and all went well. Some diamonds, a present from Mr Lorry, shone brightly on Lucie's arm. Very soon Lucie was saying goodbye to her father. For him it was a difficult parting, the first since he had come to England from France. But it was not going to be a long one; for in two weeks he would join them, and they would all three finish the holiday and return home together. At last, he removed her arms from around his neck and said, 'Take her, Charles, she is yours.'

Soon she was waving to them from the carriage window and she was gone. The Doctor, Mr Lorry and Miss Pross waved until the carriage was out of sight.

The Doctor had been very cheerful and had tried hard, and successfully, not to spoil his daughter's happiness; but something was troubling him. As he put his hand to his head and wandered around his room, Mr Lorry was reminded of the old shoemaker in the house of Monsieur Defarge.

'I think,' Mr Lorry said to Miss Pross, 'that we had better not talk to him now. I must go to Tellson's, but I will soon be back. Then we will take him out into the country for dinner, and all will be well.'

It was two hours before he came back. As he walked up the stairs towards the Doctor's room, he was stopped by a loud knocking sound.

'Good God!' he cried. 'What is that?'

Miss Pross, with a frightened expression, appeared. 'All is lost!' she cried. 'All is lost! What shall we say to Lucie? He doesn't know me and he is making shoes.'

Mr Lorry said what he could to calm Miss Pross and went inside the Doctor's room. The bench was turned towards the light as it had been in the room in Paris, his head was bent over his work, and he was very busy.

'Dr Manette. My dear friend. Dr Manette.'

The Doctor looked up for a moment – half inquiringly, half as if he were angry at being spoken to – and bent over his work again. Mr Lorry noticed that he was busy making a shoe. He took up another that was lying beside him and asked what it was.

'A young lady's walking shoe. It ought to have been finished a long time ago.'

'But, Dr Manette, look at me.'

He did as he was told, as if he was used to receiving orders.

'Don't you remember me, my dear friend? Think again. This is not your proper job. Think, my friend, think!'

But it was no good. The Doctor went on with his work and refused to say a word.

Mr Lorry decided that this must be kept a secret from Lucie and all who knew him. With the help of Miss Pross, the Doctor's friends were told that he was unwell and needed a few days' rest. As for Lucie, Miss Pross was to write and tell her that he had been called away for a few days to attend a sick patient.

Hoping that he would get better, Mr Lorry decided to watch him closely without appearing to do so. He therefore made arrangements to take a holiday from the bank for the first time in his life, and to come and live in the house.

The next day he spent in a room from which he could see the Doctor at his work. He did not attempt to speak to him, for he found that this only made the old man worse. The Doctor took

49

what was given to him to eat and drink, and worked steadily all day until it was too dark for him to see. When he had put his tools to one side, Mr Lorry rose and said to him in a natural voice, 'Will you go out?'

The Doctor looked up at him and repeated in a low voice, 'Out?'

'Yes. For a walk with me. Why not?'

The Doctor made no attempt to give a reason for not wanting to go out. He just sat with his hands to his head, and his face looked confused. He seemed to be trying to find an answer to the question, 'Why not?' But he said nothing more.

The next evening, when it fell dark, Mr Lorry asked him as before, 'Dear Doctor, will you go out?'

As before he repeated, 'Out?'

'Yes, for a walk with me. Why not?'

This time, when he refused to answer, Mr Lorry got up and pretended to go out by himself. But he only went into the next room from where he could see what happened. The Doctor got up and went to the window for a time and looked out. When he heard Mr Lorry returning, he went back to his bench.

For nine days Mr Lorry remained in the house. It was an anxious time for him; soon it would be impossible to keep the secret from Lucie any longer, and she would never forgive herself. The Doctor's hands were becoming terribly skilful at his old work as they became used to it again. On the ninth evening, Mr Lorry, worn out with watching, fell asleep in his chair and stayed there all night.

He was woken by the sun shining in at the window. Surprised at finding himself not in bed, he got up, went to the Doctor's room, and looked in. To his surprise, he saw the Doctor reading by the window. He was dressed as usual: the bench and tools had been pushed to one side.

Mr Lorry silently went away and talked with Miss Pross. They decided that they would say nothing to the Doctor, but would wait until breakfast-time and would then greet him as if nothing had happened.

This they did. The Doctor was called in the usual way and came in to breakfast. They talked about nothing in particular, but when they happened to mention the day of the week and the date, they saw him begin to count and become anxious. Then Mr Lorry decided to ask medical advice, and the person that he decided to ask was the Doctor himself.

So when the breakfast things had been cleared away, Mr Lorry began slowly, 'My dear Doctor, I am keen to have your advice on a very serious case in which I am interested. It is the case of a very dear friend of mine, so advise me well.'

'Give me all the details,' said the Doctor quietly.

'A long time ago,' said Mr Lorry, 'my friend had a great shock, and it affected his mind. He does not know for how long he remained like this, but in time he got better. He does not know what actually made him better. Unfortunately, he has recently had a return of his illness.'

'For how long?' asked the Doctor.

'For nine days and nights.'

'Does his daughter know of it?'

'No, and I hope that she never will. It was kept a secret from her. It is known only to myself and to one other who may be trusted.'

The Doctor took his hand and said, 'That was very kind of you. Thank you.'

Mr Lorry held his hand tightly in return and neither spoke for a time.

'Now, my dear Doctor, I am a man of business and am unable to deal with such matters as this. I want some good advice. And I trust you to guide me. Tell me, how did it happen? Is there danger of a return? And how should it be treated if it returns?'

The Doctor sat thinking for a time.

'I think it is possible,' he said, 'that your friend feared such a return might happen. He feared it very much. He feared it so much that he was quite unable to speak of it to any other person.'

'Now,' said Mr Lorry. 'What do you think was the cause of its return?'

'I believe,' said the other, 'that its cause was a sudden memory of the thing which caused his first illness.'

'And what can we expect for the future?'

'For the future,' went on the Doctor firmly, 'I should have great hope. As he got better so quickly, there is great hope. It will not affect him again, because what he feared has happened. The worst is over.'

'Well, we – that's a great comfort. I am thankful.'

'I, too, am thankful,' repeated the Doctor, lowering his head in thanks to God.

So the matter ended. They went out into the country and spent a pleasant day. The Doctor was quite better; on the three following days he remained perfectly well. On the fourteenth day he went away to join Lucie and her husband.

On the night of the day when he left the house, Mr Lorry went into the Doctor's room with some workmen's tools. Soon the noise of hammering and wood breaking came from the room, and the sound of someone dragging big pieces of wood to the fireplace. The wood was thrown into the fire and the flames began to rise high. Some half-finished shoes and pieces of leather followed the wood, and they too were soon burning brightly. Then Mr Lorry dug a hole in the garden and Miss Pross threw into it various tools.

There was now no sign of the shoemaker of Paris.

Chapter 13   Revolution

When Lucie and her husband returned home, one of the first visitors was Sydney Carton, and as time passed he remained a visitor, though an infrequent one, coming about six times a year. As time passed, too, the house rang to the happy sound of a child's laughter, and whenever Sydney Carton came to see his friends, it was noticed that little Lucie seemed to like him.

Another and more frequent visitor was Mr Lorry. One night in mid-July 1789, he came in late from Tellson's and sat down by Lucie and her husband in the dark window.

'I began to think,' he said, 'that I should have to pass the night at Tellson's. We have had so much business all day that we didn't know what to do first. There is such anxiety in Paris that the people there are putting their property in our hands and sending it to England as fast as they can.'

'That looks bad,' said Darnay.

'Yes, but we don't know the reason for it. Where is Manette?'

'Here he is,' said the Doctor, entering the room at that moment. 'Will you have a game of cards with me?'

'I don't think I will tonight. I am too tired. But I will have some tea, if Lucie will give me some.'

'Of course,' said Lucie.

'Thank you, my dear. Is the child safely in bed?'

'Yes, and fast asleep.'

'That's good; all safe and well. I don't know why anything should not be safe and well here, thank God. But I have been so troubled all day that I am not my usual self. I am not so young as I was! My tea, my dear! Thank you. Now let us sit quietly and talk.'

♦

That same day, far away in Saint-Antoine, a great roar rose from the throats of the people and a forest of arms struggled in the air like the branches of trees in a winter wind. All the fingers were holding weapons: guns, bars of wood and iron, knives and any other thing that would serve. People who could find nothing else set themselves with bleeding fingers to pull stones and bricks out of walls. The centre of this roaring crowd was Defarge's wine shop. There Defarge himself was giving out arms and orders.

'Keep near me, Jacques Three,' he cried. 'And you, Jacques One and Two, separate, and put yourselves at the head of as many of these patriots as you can. Where is my wife?'

'Here I am,' said Madame, as calm as ever, but not knitting today. 'I am going with you for the moment. But soon you will see me at the head of the women.'

'Come, then, friends and patriots!' cried Defarge. 'We are ready. To the Bastille!'

With a roar the living sea rose, wave after wave, and overflowed the city to the Bastille. Fire and smoke soon covered the thick stone walls, and the eight great towers. In the middle of the fire and smoke was Defarge. 'Work, friends, work!' he cried. 'Work, Jacques One, Jacques Two, Jacques One Thousand, Jacques Twenty-Five Thousand.'

'Come to me!' cried his wife to the women. 'We can kill as well as the men when the place is taken.' And to her came the women, differently armed, but all armed by hunger and revenge in the same way.

Suddenly a white flag was raised inside the Bastille, and Defarge was swept by the crowd through the gates of the prison. He had no time to turn his head or look around him until he found himself in the outer courtyard. Everywhere was noise, shouting and cheering.

'The prisoners!'

'The records!'

'The secret cells!'

The crowd seized the prison officers and threatened them with immediate death if they did not take them immediately to every secret part of the prison. Defarge seized one of them himself.

'Show me the North Tower!' said Defarge. 'Quick!'

'I will, I will,' cried the man, 'if you will come with me. But there is no one there.'

'What is the meaning of One Hundred and Five, North Tower?'

'It is a cell.'

'Show it to me!'

'Come this way then.'

Through dark stone halls where the light of day had never shone, past the ugly doors of small dark rooms and cages, down wet stone steps, Defarge and Jacques Three, who went with him, were led by the prison officer. Because of the thickness of the walls, the noise of the shouting crowd soon died away.

'One Hundred and Five, North Tower!'

There was a small window, with bars across it but without glass, high up in the wall. There was a small chimney, also heavily barred. There was a small wooden seat, a table and a wooden bed. There were the four blackened walls, and a big old iron ring in one of them.

'Pass the light along these walls, so that I may see them,' said Defarge.

The man did as he was asked.

'Stop! Look here, Jacques!'

'A. M.' read Jacques.

'Alexandre Manette,' said Defarge in his ear. 'And here he wrote "A poor doctor". Give me that iron bar!'

Turning to the wooden seat and the table, he beat them to pieces with a few blows.

'Look carefully among the pieces, Jacques. And see! Here is my knife. Cut open that bed and search it. Hold the light higher!'

Defarge himself examined the chimney, bringing down some dirt and dust and searching with his fingers in the chimney itself and in the old wood ashes that lay below.

'Nothing in the bed, Jacques?'

'Nothing.'

'Let us collect them and burn them. Light them, you!'

The man set fire to the little pile and, leaving it burning, they went out again through the low door. So they came back to the courtyard and the shouting.

The crowd had seized the governor of the prison and was marching him away to judgement. Near him walked Madame Defarge, and when her husband appeared, she called to him. She stayed near the frightened governor as they went along, and when he was struck from behind and fell dead, she put her foot on his neck and cut off his head.

So the revolution began and so it continued. Saint-Antoine's day had come and Saint-Antoine was angry. They hanged men on lamp-posts in the street. They set free the prisoners from the Bastille and carried the surprised men on their shoulders through the streets. In everything they did they were merciless, for they had been hardened in the fires of suffering and the touch of pity could make no mark on them.

Chapter 14   The End of the Castle

The village where Gaspard had been put to death was a poor one. Around it the countryside lay in ruins. Everything seemed tired and broken – houses, fences, animals, men, women and children, and even the land that gave them their living. For very many years, the family of the late Marquis had taken money from it by means of such people as Monsieur Gabelle, the tax collector. Now there was nothing left to be taken and hardly enough to support the miserable people who lived in it. The people were the same, though the Marquis had gone. There were in addition some strangers living in the village, strangers whose work lay in teaching the simple people new ideas and in leading them when the new ideas were put into operation.

The prison on the hill, from which Gaspard had been led to his death, was just the same. There were still soldiers in it, and officers over the soldiers. But not one of the officers knew what his men would do, except that they would probably not do what they were ordered. The new ideas had spread from Paris to the towns, and from the towns to the villages, and were now spreading to the soldiers.

The roadmender still continued his old work, though in return for his work he received hardly enough to keep him alive. Often, as he worked, he was passed by rough strangers, on foot, in wooden shoes, armed. These strangers were spreading the new ideas through the whole country and were carrying out orders given to them by the revolutionary leaders in Paris.

Such a stranger walked up to the roadmender one day in July on the road that ran over the hill outside the village. The man looked at the roadmender, at the village below, at the church and at the prison beyond. He appeared to have found what he was looking for.

'How goes it, Jacques?' he said.

'All well, Jacques.'

The man sat down on a pile of stones.

'No dinner?'

'Nothing but supper now,' replied the roadmender.

'It is the same everywhere,' said the man. 'I meet people everywhere who have had no dinner.'

He took out a blackened pipe, filled it, lit it, and then smoked until the tobacco grew red. Then he took it from his mouth and dropped something in it that burst into a little flame and went out.

The roadmender recognized a signal which he had been expecting.

'Tonight?' he asked.

'Tonight. The others will meet me here. Where is the place?'

'Along the road, about 5 miles the other side of the village.'

'Good. When do you stop work?'

'At sunset.'

'Will you wake me before you leave? I have been walking for two nights without rest. Let me finish my pipe and I shall sleep like a child. Don't forget to wake me.'

The stranger finished his pipe, put it away, took off his great wooden shoes and lay down on his back against the stones. He fell asleep immediately.

He slept all afternoon. Then when the sun was low in the west and the sky was red, the roadmender collected his tools together and woke him.

'Good,' said the sleeper, getting up. 'About 5 miles beyond the village?'

'About that.'

The roadmender went down into the village square and whispered to several of the villagers. They whispered to others. Later, when the villagers had eaten their miserable supper, they did not go to bed as usual, but came out of doors again and remained there whispering in the square. As they whispered, all eyes were turned to the sky, but in one direction only.

Monsieur Gabelle became uneasy. He went to the top of his house and looked in that direction too. He sent word to the man who kept the keys of the church that there might be a need to ring the church bells soon.

The darkness deepened. The wind rose. The trees that kept guard round the old castle moved in the rising wind and bent their heads towards the huge building. Four rough figures made their way through the trees and came into the courtyard. Four lights appeared and then separated, each one going in a different direction. Then everything was dark again.

But not for long. Soon the castle seemed to shine through the night by means of some strange light of its own. The windows shone; smoke rose and flames climbed high and grew broader and brighter. Soon the whole of the front of the castle could be seen in the heart of roaring flames.

Soon a horseman came riding into the village through the darkness and pulled up at Monsieur Gabelle's door.

'Help, Gabelle! Help, everyone!'

The church bells rang out, calling the people. But no one moved. The mender of roads, with 200 particular friends, stood with folded arms in the square looking at the fire in the sky over the castle.

'It must be 40 feet high,' one said and laughed, and nobody moved.

The rider from the castle rode away through the village and up the hill to the prison. At the gate, a group of officers were looking at the fire; a short distance away a large group of soldiers were doing the same thing.

'Help, gentlemen! The castle is on fire. Valuable things may still be saved from the flames. Help! Help!'

The officers looked towards the soldiers, who looked towards the fire. They gave no orders, knowing that nobody would listen. They answered, 'It must burn.'

The castle was left to the flames. The wind blew the fire, and soon great pieces of stone and wood fell. The nearest trees grew hot, dropped their leaves and began to smoke. Birds flew around, and many of them, made helpless by the heat and the smoke, dropped into the flames. Four men walked away into the night, north, south, east and west, each to another castle. Down in the village the church bells were ringing again. But not, this time, to warn the villagers about anything; this time they were being rung for joy.

Not only that. The villagers, excited by the fire, by the bell-ringing and by hunger, remembered that it was Monsieur Gabelle who used to collect the rent and the taxes, though little rent and very few taxes had been collected in recent times. They surrounded his house and shouted to him to come out. Hearing this, Gabelle barred his door heavily and hid on the top of his house, behind the chimneys. There, being a brave man, he decided that if they burst in his door, he would throw himself head first off the roof into the middle of them and in this way take perhaps one or two of them with him to the next world.

But the excitement of the villagers died down, and when the first light of day appeared in the sky, the people went home; and Monsieur Gabelle came down again, thankful to be still alive.

That night, and on other nights, other officials in other villages were not as fortunate as Monsieur Gabelle. In the morning they were found hanging from trees in once-peaceful forests. In some villages, the soldiers attacked the people and hanged a few of them in their turn. But wherever the four men went, north, south, east or west, fire broke out, and terror walked the night.

Chapter 15   Business in Paris

The meeting place in London for all the rich people who had escaped from France was, of course, Tellson's Bank. Those who had had the good sense to send their money to England before the revolution went to the bank for business purposes; and those who had not, went there hoping to meet old friends who might be able and ready to help them out of their difficulties. Tellson's became at that time a centre where one could learn the latest news from France. This was well known to the public, and many inquiries were made there. As a result, the news was sometimes written out and put in the bank window for all to see.

One afternoon, half an hour before closing time, Mr Lorry was sitting at his desk and Charles Darnay stood leaning on it and talking to him in a low voice.

'You think I am too old to go?' said Mr Lorry.

'Unsettled weather, a long journey, uncertain means of travelling, a city that may not be safe—'

'My dear Charles, it is safe enough for me. Nobody will trouble an old man of nearly eighty, when there are so many others to trouble. Besides, it is necessary for someone to go from our bank here to our bank there, somebody who knows the city and the business. For Tellson's, after all these years, I ought to go.'

'I wish I were going myself,' said Darnay, like a man thinking out loud.

'Really! You wish you were going yourself! But you are a Frenchman!'

'My dear Mr Lorry, it is because I am a Frenchman that the thought has often crossed my mind. I sometimes think that I might be able to persuade the people not to be so violent.'

'And what about Lucie? You should be ashamed of yourself, wishing you were going to France!'

'Well, I am not going,' said Darnay with a smile. 'But you say that you are.'

'Yes, I am really going. You can have no idea, Charles, of the difficulty of doing business at present, or of the danger to our books and papers in France. They may be seized or destroyed at any moment. If I go, I may be able to save some of the more important ones, or bury them, or somehow get them out of harm's way. Hardly anyone but myself can do it. Shouldn't I go?'

'How I admire you! So you are really going tonight?'

'Tonight. We must not wait any longer.'

'Will you take anyone with you?'

'I intend to take Jerry. He will look after me. Then, when I have done this little piece of business, perhaps I shall accept Tellson's offer to let me finish work and live out my life quietly.'

This conversation took place at Mr Lorry's usual desk; near the desk stood many of the rich French aristocrats who had come to the bank on business. Among these men was also Stryver, who was explaining how he would blow up all the people of France, and remove them from the face of the earth. Darnay heard all that he said with particular displeasure. Just then, the head of the bank came up to them and laid a dirty and unopened letter before Mr Lorry, asking whether he had found any sign of the man to whom it was addressed yet. The letter was placed so close to Darnay that he saw the address, which ran: 'Very urgent. To the former Marquis St Evrémonde, of France, care of Tellson & Co., Bankers, London, England.'

On the morning of the wedding Dr Manette had begged Darnay not to tell anyone else his real name, unless the Doctor first agreed. So no one else, not even his wife or Mr Lorry, knew who he really was.

'No,' said Mr Lorry, in reply to the director. 'I have asked everyone here, but no one can tell me where this gentleman may be found.'

He held out the letter so that those standing near might see it.

'The son of the brother of the Marquis who was murdered,' said one. 'I am happy to say that I never knew him.'

'An animal who ran away and left his post,' said another.

'A man who has come under the influence of the new ideas,' said a third. 'He quarrelled with the last Marquis and then left the property to the mercy of the people.'

'What?' shouted Stryver. 'Is that the sort of person? Let me see the man's name.'

Darnay was unable to keep silent any longer. 'I know the man,' he said.

'Do you?' said Stryver. 'I am sorry to hear it. It is better not to know such a man. He is worthless. If he is a gentleman, I don't understand him. You may tell him so from me. You may also tell him from me that, as he left his property to the revolutionaries, I am surprised that he is not at the head of them. But no; of course not. Such a man would not trust himself to them. He would always run away.'

With these words, Stryver, with a last wave of his arm, walked out, followed by most of those who had been listening. Mr Lorry and Darnay were left alone at the desk.

'Will you take charge of the letter?' said Mr Lorry. 'Do you know where to deliver it?'

'I do.'

'Will you explain why it has been here for some time?'

'I will do so. Do you start your journey to Paris from here?'

'From here at eight.'

'I will come back to see you before you go.'

Anxious and confused, Darnay took the letter and left. As soon as he reached a quiet place, he opened it and read it. It was as follows:

PRISON OF THE ABBAYE,
PARIS
June 21st, 1792

Monsieur,
After having long been in danger of my life at the hands of the villagers, I have been seized and brought on foot to Paris. Nor is that

all; my house has been completely destroyed.

The crime for which I am in prison, and for which I shall be tried, and shall lose my life (without your help), is that I have acted for one who has left his country. To say that I acted for the people and not against them has no effect; those were your orders. It is useless to say that I did not collect the taxes, and that I did not ask for the rent, that I did not go to law. I ask 'Of what am I accused?' The only answer that I receive is that I acted for an émigré★, and where is he?

Ah, Monsieur! Where is he? I ask in my sleep where he is. I ask Heaven whether he will come to set me free. No answer. Ah, Monsieur! I send my sad cry across the sea, hoping that it may reach your ears through the great Bank of Tellson, known in Paris. For the love of God, I beg you, Monsieur, to help me and to set me free. My fault is that I have been true to you. I pray that you will be true to me.

From this prison of terror, where death comes nearer and nearer,

Your unfortunate,

GABELLE.

Darnay was very upset by this letter. He had told Gabelle to do his best for the people and to give them what little there was to give. Now his trusted servant was in prison and his only crime was that he had carried out orders.

It seemed quite clear to Darnay that he must go to Paris. He saw no danger. He thought the people of France would be grateful for what he had done, even though it had been done imperfectly. Perhaps he would be able to save his old servant from the death that now seemed certain.

As he walked up and down, thinking what ought to be done, he decided that neither Lucie nor her father must know that he was going until after he had actually gone. It would be best to

---

★ **émigré** (a French word, also used in English): someone who has left their country for political reasons

keep his intentions to himself in order to protect others from anxiety, if possible. With these thoughts in his mind he returned to say goodbye to Mr Lorry.

'I have delivered the letter,' he said. 'There is no written answer, but perhaps you will take a spoken one?'

'Certainly,' said Mr Lorry.

'It is to a prisoner in the Abbaye; his name is Gabelle.'

'Gabelle.'

'The message is, "He has received the letter and will come." '

'Is any time mentioned?'

'He will start on his journey tomorrow night.'

'Very well,' said Mr Lorry. 'And now I must go. Give my love to Lucie, and to little Lucie, and take care of them until I come back.'

Charles Darnay shook his head and smiled doubtfully as the carriage moved away.

That night – it was the fourteenth of August – he sat up late and wrote two letters, to be delivered after he had gone, one to Lucie and one to the Doctor, explaining the matter to both of them and saying that he would write to them from France.

The next day was a difficult one, as he had to spend it with them without telling them of his plans. Early in the evening he kissed his wife and daughter and went out, pretending that he would soon return. And so, with a heavy heart, he began his journey, encouraged by the thought that he was going to help a poor prisoner anxiously waiting for him across the sea.

Chapter 16   Darnay Returns to France

In the year 1792 it took a long time to travel from England to Paris. Even at the time of King Louis the roads, the carriages and the horses in France were bad. But now there were other difficulties. Every town and village had its band of "patriots", all armed with loaded guns, who stopped all comers and all goers, questioned them, examined their papers, looked for their names in lists of their own, turned them back, sent them on, or took them in, just as they liked, all in the name of "Liberty, Equality and Fraternity" and of the new Republic of France.

Charles Darnay had not gone very far along the country roads when he began to realize that he would never be allowed to return until he was recognized as a good citizen by the people of Paris. Whatever might happen, he must go on to his journey's end. Every gate that closed behind him, he knew to be another gate that shut him away from his loved ones in England. He felt like an animal in a net, like a bird in a cage, so complete was his loss of liberty.

Twenty times in a single day he was stopped, questioned, taken back or sent forward. He had been on the roads of France for three days and was still a long way from Paris. He went to bed, tired out, in a small hotel. It was only by showing Gabelle's letter that he had been able to come so far. He was not at all surprised when he was woken in the middle of the night by an official and three armed patriots.

'Émigré,' said the official, 'I am going to send you on to Paris with a guard of soldiers to see that you get there.'

'Citizen, I desire nothing more than to get to Paris; but I do not need the soldiers.'

'Silence,' said one of the armed men, striking the bed with the end of his gun. 'Be quiet, aristocrat!'

'It is as the good patriot says,' remarked the official. 'You are an aristocrat. You must have a guard, and must pay for it. Rise and dress yourself, émigré.'

Darnay had to do what they ordered. He was taken to a guard house where other rough patriots were smoking, drinking and sleeping around a fire. Here he had to pay a heavy price for his

66

guard, and started along the wet roads at three o'clock in the morning.

The guard consisted of two patriots with red caps, both armed, who rode on either side of him. One of them tied a rope to Darnay's horse and kept the other end tied to his arm. In this way they travelled on. Fear filled Darnay's breast, but he hoped that all would be well when Gabelle told the patriots why he had come back.

At the town of Beauvais he found himself in real danger. An angry crowd surrounded him shouting, 'Down with the émigré!' He attempted to explain himself.

'Émigré, my friends! I am here of my own free will.'

'You are a dirty émigré,' shouted a man, coming towards him with a hammer in his hand. 'And you are a dirty aristocrat.'

Placing himself between the man and Darnay, an official said, 'Leave him alone. Leave him alone. He will be judged in Paris.'

'Yes!' cried another. 'He'll be judged! Yes! Judged and punished as an enemy of France.'

'Friend,' said Darnay, 'I am not an enemy.'

'He lies,' the man shouted. 'Under the new law his life and property belong to the government.'

But Darnay did not feel safe until his guards had managed to get him into the courtyard of a hotel and had closed the door on the angry crowd.

'What is this new law?' he asked.

'It is a new law punishing with death all émigrés who return. It was passed on the fourteenth of this month.'

'The day I left England!'

After a short rest, and many hours of miserable travel, they found themselves at last at a road block outside the walls of Paris. The road was closed and strongly guarded as they rode up and stopped. A determined-looking man came out of the guard house; he seemed to be in charge there.

'Where are the papers of this prisoner?' he demanded.

'Prisoner!' said Darnay angrily. 'I am a free traveller. I am a French citizen. I have come back to France of my own free will and I am travelling with these guards, for whose services I have paid.'

The man took no notice of him at all.

'Where are the papers of this prisoner?' he repeated.

One of the patriots produced the papers. The man looked at the papers and read the letter. Then without saying a word he went back into the guard house while they sat on their horses, waiting. Darnay looked around him as they waited. He saw a great crowd of men, women, animals and carts, all waiting to come out. But, as everyone was very closely examined, they had to wait a long time. Some, knowing that their turn would take a long time, were lying on the ground trying to sleep. Others talked together, or just waited silently. Everybody, whether man or woman, was wearing a red cap.

After a long time a man came out and ordered a soldier to open the gate. Then he gave the patriots a paper to say the prisoner had been received safely, and ordered him to get down from the horse. He obeyed, and the patriots, leading his tired horse, turned and rode away without entering the city.

Darnay was taken into the guard house. A number of soldiers and patriots, smelling strongly of wine and tobacco, were standing or lying about. Some large books were lying open on a desk, and an officer of a rough, dark appearance, was looking into them.

'Citizen Defarge,' said the officer to the man who had brought Darnay in, 'Citizen Defarge, is this the émigré, Evrémonde?'

'This is the man,' answered Defarge.

'Your age, Evrémonde?'

'Thirty-seven.'

'Married, Evrémonde?'

'Yes.'

'Where is your wife?'

'In England.'

'No doubt! You are to be taken, Evrémonde, to the prison of La Force.'

'By God!' cried Darnay. 'Under what law, and for what crime?'

'We have new laws, Evrémonde, since the last time you were here.' He said the words with a hard smile and went on writing.

'I beg you to make a note that I came here of my own free will, in answer to that letter that lies before you, a letter from a respected citizen. Have I no rights?'

'Émigrés have no rights, Evrémonde,' was the reply.

The officer read over to himself what he had written and handed it to Defarge with the words 'In secret'.

Defarge told the prisoner to go with him. A guard of two patriots attended them.

'Is it you,' said Defarge, as they went down the steps of the guard house and turned into Paris, 'is it you who married the daughter of Dr Manette?'

'Yes,' said Darnay, looking at him in surprise.

'My name is Defarge, and I keep a wine shop in Saint-Antoine. Perhaps you have heard of me?'

'Yes. My wife came to your house to reclaim her father.'

'And what has brought you back to France?'

'You heard me say the reason a minute ago. Don't you believe that it is the truth?'

'A bad truth for you,' said Defarge.

'You're right. I feel lost here. All is so unexpected, so changed, so unfair. I feel completely lost. Will you do something for me?'

'Nothing.'

'In the prison to which you are taking me, shall I not be able to get any message to the outside world? Shall I be judged without any means of defending myself?'

'You will see. But suppose you are – other people have been sent to worse prisons before now.'

'It is of the greatest importance to me that I should be able to send a message to Mr Lorry of Tellson's Bank who is now in Paris. Will you please do this for me? Just tell Mr Lorry that I have been thrown into the prison of La Force.'

'I will do nothing for you. My duty is to my country and my people. I am your enemy. I will do nothing to help you.'

Darnay felt that it was hopeless to ask again and they walked on in silence. Their passing through the streets attracted no attention. A well-dressed person going to prison had become as common a sight as a worker going to his work. Even the children hardly noticed them. A few people turned their heads to look, and a few shouted insults at him for being an aristocrat, but otherwise no notice was taken. At a street corner a man was addressing a small crowd and Darnay heard his words as he passed. He learned that the King had been taken to prison and that the representatives of foreign governments had all left Paris.

The prison of La Force was a dark and ugly place. An evil smell seemed to fill it. Defarge handed over his prisoner to the head guard of the prison with the words, 'The émigré, Evrémonde.'

'What the devil! How many more of them?' said the guard.

He gave Defarge a paper in exchange for his prisoner.

'What the devil, I say again,' he said to his wife. 'How many more?'

His wife replied, 'We must have patience, my dear, for the love of freedom.'

' "In secret", too,' he continued. 'And almost every place full.'

He rang a bell and three men came in. They all looked at Darnay, studied him carefully and for a long time so that his appearance should be printed on their memory.

'Come!' said the man, taking up his keys. 'Come with me, émigré.'

Down passages and up stone stairways they went, through doors that were unlocked to let them through and locked again behind them, until they came to a large, low room, crowded with prisoners, both men and women. The women were all seated round a large table, knitting or sewing; the men were standing behind them or were walking slowly up and down the room. Here were some of the richest and oldest families of France. Even in misfortune and misery, they still kept their fine manners and behaved in prison, as far as they could, just as they used to behave in their great castles.

A gentleman of fine appearance and manner came forward and said, 'I have the honour of welcoming you to La Force. I am sorry that you have come among us. May your stay here end soon, and happily! Will you please tell us your name?'

Darnay gave the information.

'But I hope,' said the gentleman, following the prison guard with his eyes, 'that you are not "in secret".'

'I do not understand the meaning of it exactly, but I have heard them say so.'

'Ah, what a pity. We are so sorry. But take courage. Several members of our society have been "in secret", but it lasted only a short time.'

Then he added, raising his voice, 'I am sorry to inform the company that the new prisoner is "in secret".'

Darnay crossed the room to where a guard was waiting for him. They passed through a door which he locked behind him and then climbed some stone stairs. He opened a low black door and they passed into a small empty cell. It was cold and wet, but not dark.

'Yours,' said the man.

'Why am I to be locked up alone?'

'How do I know?'

'Can I buy pens, ink and paper?'

'Such are not my orders. You will be visited and may ask then. At present you may buy your food, and nothing else.'

There were in the cell a chair, a table and a bed, which the guard examined before he went out.

Darnay heard the key turning in the lock. He was alone in La Force.

Chapter 17   Mr Lorry in Paris

When Mr Lorry reached Paris, he took rooms in Tellson's Bank in that city, so as to be able to carry out his business more easily. One night he was sitting by the fire when the door of the room was suddenly thrown open, and two figures rushed in. Their appearance was so unexpected that he was filled with surprise.

'Lucie! Manette! What is the matter? What has happened?'

'Oh, my dear husband!' cried Lucie. 'My husband!'

'Your husband, Lucie?'

'He is here in Paris! He has been here for three or four days. He came to help someone. He has been put in prison.'

The old man gave a cry. Almost at the same moment, the bell of the great gate outside rang, and the noise of feet and voices came pouring into the courtyard.

'What is that noise?' said the Doctor, turning towards the window.

'Don't look out!' cried Mr Lorry. 'For your life, do not let them see you!'

'My dear friend,' said Dr Manette, 'I have been a prisoner in the Bastille. I am safe here. Anyone who knows of my time in prison will do anything for me. My sufferings have given me power now. They brought us into the city and gave us news of Charles. I knew it would be so. I knew I could save Charles. What is that noise?'

'Don't look!' repeated Mr Lorry. 'Nor you, Lucie, my dear. Where is Charles?'

'In the prison of La Force!'

'La Force! Lucie, you must do just what I tell you. You can do nothing tonight. You must stay quietly in a room at the back here, and leave your father and me alone for a few minutes.'

'I will do what you say. I trust you.'

The old man kissed her, then he hurried her into the room and turned the key. He returned to the Doctor and the two looked carefully out of the window into the courtyard. They saw 40 or 50 people sharpening knives, swords and other weapons on a big stone. The faces of these men and women were wild and violent, and marked with blood.

'They are murdering the prisoners,' whispered Mr Lorry. 'If you are sure of your power, tell these people who you are and go to La Force. It may be too late now, but let it not be a minute later!'

Dr Manette pressed Mr Lorry's hand and hurried out. He was in the courtyard when Mr Lorry went back to the window. The Doctor's white hair, his remarkable face and the confidence of his manner carried him immediately into the middle of the crowd. For a moment there was a pause. Then Mr Lorry saw him hurry out, surrounded by all the people shouting, 'Long live the Bastille prisoner! Help for his friend in La Force! Save the prisoner Evrémonde in La Force!'

Mr Lorry left the window and, hurrying to Lucie, told her what had happened. He found her child and Miss Pross in the entrance hall. Through the long night they waited for news but none came. By midday the next day there was still no message, and Mr Lorry began to feel that Lucie should not stay any longer in the bank; his duty was to Tellson's and he had no right to bring any difficulties in the way of the bank, even to help his friends. When he mentioned the matter to Lucie, she said that her father had intended to rent some rooms near the bank.

He immediately took Lucie, her child and Miss Pross to these rooms, giving them what comfort he could and much more than he had himself. He left Jerry with them to take care of them, and returned to the bank, where he worked until it closed at the end of the day. When he was once more alone in his room, he heard a foot upon the stairs. In a few moments a man stood before him who addressed him by his name.

'That is my name,' said Mr Lorry. 'Do you know me?'

'Do you know me?' answered the man.

'I have seen you somewhere.'

'Perhaps at my wine shop?'

'Have you come from Dr Manette?' asked Mr Lorry, both interested and worried.

'Yes.'

Defarge gave him a piece of paper with some words in the Doctor's writing:

Charles is safe but I cannot leave this place yet. The man who brings this has a short note from Charles to his wife. Let the man see her.

'Will you come with me,' said Mr Lorry joyfully, 'to where his wife lives?'

'Yes,' answered Defarge.

Mr Lorry hardly noticed that Defarge spoke coldly. They went down into the courtyard, where they found two women, one knitting.

'Madame Defarge, surely!' said Mr Lorry. 'Is she coming with us?'

'Yes, so she may be able to recognize the persons. It is for their safety.'

Mr Lorry looked doubtfully at Defarge, and led the way. Both the women followed. The second woman was called The Revenge.

Jerry let them in and they found Lucie alone. She was full of joy to hear the news and pressed the hand that delivered the note.

Dearest – Take courage. I am well and your father has influence here. You cannot answer this. Kiss our child for me.

That was all the writing, but it was much to her who received it. She kissed the hand of Madame Defarge, but it felt cold and heavy. There was something in its touch that made Lucie pause and look at the woman in terror.

'My dear,' explained Mr Lorry, 'there are many fights in the streets, and Madame Defarge wants to see you so that she may know you in future and be able to help you if necessary. Is that right, Citizen Defarge?'

The three heard these words in stony silence.

'You had better ask Miss Pross to bring the child here,' continued Mr Lorry, 'so that they may see her, too.'

When Miss Pross brought little Lucie in, Madame Defarge asked:

'Is that his child?'

'Yes, Madame,' said Mr Lorry.

'It is enough, husband,' said Madame Defarge. 'We may go.'

'You will be good to my husband? You will let me see him if you can?' said Lucie.

'Your husband is not my business here,' answered Madame.

'As a wife and a mother, I beg you to have pity on me, and to do your best for my husband, who is guilty of no crime.'

75

'What about all the wives and mothers we have seen since we were children? We have known their husbands and fathers put in prison often enough. All our lives we have seen them suffer in hunger, sickness and misery.'

'We have seen nothing else,' said The Revenge.

'We have borne this a long time,' said Madame Defarge. 'Do you think it likely that the trouble of one wife and mother would be much to us now?'

She started knitting again and went out, followed by the other two.

'Courage, my dear,' said Mr Lorry. 'We are better off than many other poor souls. Be thankful.'

'I am not ungrateful, I hope,' said Lucie. 'But that terrible woman seems to throw a shadow on me and on all my hopes.'

Although Mr Lorry did his best to be cheerful, he was also secretly deeply troubled.

Four days passed after Dr Manette went to La Force. Then he returned. He did not tell Lucie that, during that time, 1,100 defenceless men and women, prisoners of all ages, had been killed by the people. She only knew that there had been an attack on the prisons and that some of the prisoners had been murdered. But he told Mr Lorry, under a promise of secrecy, what had happened.

Dr Manette had found a kind of court sitting at the prison. He had declared himself to be a Bastille prisoner. Defarge had recognized him. Then the Doctor had asked that Darnay should be examined immediately, and the court had agreed. For some reason (which the Doctor could not understand) they had refused to set Darnay free, but they had agreed that he should be kept safe in prison and not put to death. The Doctor had remained to watch over him until the people became calmer and the danger was over.

As the Doctor described the terrible sights he had seen in the prison, Mr Lorry began to fear that such experiences might bring back the old illness. But the days passed, and it became clear that the Doctor had received strength and power from his suffering. 'My time in prison,' he said, 'was not just waste and ruin, my friend. As my dear child helped me to get better, I will now bring back her husband to her side. With the help of Heaven, I will do it!' And when Jarvis saw the determined face and calm look with which the Doctor went around the city, he believed him.

The Doctor used his influence so wisely that he soon became the medical officer of three prisons, including La Force. In this way he was able to see Darnay every week and to bring Lucie news of him. But though he tried to get him set free, or at least to get him brought to trial, the events of the time were too strong for him. The new age began; the King was tried and put to death; the black flag waved from the great towers of Notre-Dame (the most important church in Paris); the prisons were filled with people who had done no wrong; and the guillotine struck down the powerful and killed the beautiful and the good. Among all these terrors walked the Doctor with a steady head, never doubting that he would save Lucie's husband in the end.

Chapter 18   Darnay's Trial

One year and three months passed. For all this time Lucie was never sure, from hour to hour, that the guillotine would not cut off her husband's head the next day. Every day carts passed through the stony streets, filled with people on their way to die under the cruel knife of the guillotine. Lovely girls, gentle women, black-haired, brown-haired and grey; young men and old, poor men and aristocrats, all were brought out from terrible prisons each day and carried through the streets to feed the guillotine. The hunger of the guillotine could not be satisfied.

Liberty, Equality, Fraternity – or Death: and of these four, death was by far the commonest.

This was a hard time for Lucie. If she had given way to hopelessness, she could not have lived. But she kept herself busy. She looked after her father and her daughter as she had done in England. She taught little Lucie her lessons just as regularly as if they were all safe at home in England. And she had good reason for hope, since Dr Manette was a loved and respected figure among the revolutionaries. Whenever she expressed her fears and anxieties to him, he always answered firmly:

'Nothing can happen to Charles without my knowledge, and I know that I can save him, Lucie.'

One day her father said to her, on coming home, 'My dear, there is an upper window in the prison which Charles can sometimes get to. When he gets to it (and this is not often), he might see you in the street if you stand in a certain place which I can show you. But you will not be able to see him, my poor child. And even if you could, it would be dangerous for you to make any sign that you recognize him.'

'Oh, show me the place, Father, and I will go there every day.'

The place was the corner of a dark and dirty street, near the woodcutter's hut. From that time, in all weathers, she waited for two hours at that place. When the clock struck two, she was there; and at four she turned sadly away. In fine weather she took little Lucie with her; in bad weather she waited alone, but she never missed a single day.

The woodcutter had formerly been a roadmender, but was now earning his living by cutting wood into lengths for burning. After seeing her several times, always in the same place, he greeted her.

'Good day, citizeness.'

'Good day, citizen,' she replied.

He guessed why she came. He pointed at the prison, put his

fingers in front of his face like the bars on the windows and looked through them as a prisoner would.

'But it's not my business,' he said, and went on cutting wood.

The next day Lucie brought her daughter to the spot, and the woodcutter saw her again. He showed the child his tools, and one which he called his little guillotine, and showed her how it cut off pieces of wood just as the real guillotine cut off people's heads. Lucie was filled with terror, but she dared not quarrel with him. Instead, she gave him money, because she could not wait in any other place and she was afraid of him. Sometimes she saw him watching her, and when she looked at him, he used to repeat, 'It's not my business,' and go on cutting wood.

In all weathers, in the snow of winter, in the bitter winds of spring, in the hot sunshine of summer, and in the rains of autumn, Lucie spent two hours every day at the spot. Her husband saw her (so she learned from her father) about once every five times. Sometimes he saw her one day after another; at other times he did not see her for a whole week or more.

One day in December, as she was waiting in her usual place, her father came to her.

'Lucie, I have just left Charles. He is going to the window. There is no one here to see you, so you may kiss your hand to him and he will see you.'

Lucie kissed her hand several times in the direction of the prison.

'You cannot see him, can you, my dear?'

'No, Father; I cannot.'

There was a footstep in the snow. They turned and found a woman passing close to them. It was Madame Defarge.

'I greet you, citizeness,' said the Doctor.

'I greet you, citizen,' replied Madame Defarge, and passed, like a dark shadow, along the white road.

'Give me your arm, Lucie, and let us go in from here with an air of cheerfulness and courage – for him. Good! That was well done. You held your head up bravely. He will be proud of you. Now listen. I have important news. Charles will be called for trial tomorrow: he will be tried at the Conciergerie.'★

'Tomorrow!'

'Are you afraid?'

'I trust in you,' she replied, shaking.

'Trust in me,' said the Doctor. 'Your long wait is nearly ended, my love. He will be brought back to you in a few hours. Now I must see Lorry.'

Old Mr Lorry was still at his bank. He had never left it. His books were often examined by officials searching for the property of émigrés. What he could save for the owners, he saved. He was the best man that Tellson's could have sent to France during these difficult times.

There was a visitor with Mr Lorry, a visitor who did not want to be seen. This visitor, hearing the arrival of the Doctor and Lucie, quickly got up and hid himself in another room. It was Sydney Carton. He heard Mr Lorry welcome Lucie and her father, and heard him repeat the words:

'Removed to the Conciergerie and called for tomorrow.'

Every evening, a list of names was read out in the prison and in every other prison. They were the names of those who were to be removed to the Conciergerie for trial the next morning.

Charles Darnay, who was no longer "in secret", had heard the list read out many times. He had heard hundreds of names read out and seen hundreds pass away, never to return. Then at last he heard his own name.

'Charles Evrémonde, called Darnay.'

There were twenty-three names, but only twenty replied; one

★ **Conciergerie**: a prison in France during the French Revolution.

of the persons named had died in prison and been forgotten, and two had already gone to the guillotine.

Darnay stepped forward with the others whose names had been called. He spoke a few words to some of the others, but the parting was soon over. In fact, such partings were so common that no one paid much attention to them. They were just part of prison life.

The passage to the Conciergerie was short and dark. The night in its wet cells was long and cold. The next day 15 prisoners were taken out and tried before Charles Darnay was called. The trials of the whole fifteen occupied one hour and a half. All 15 were sent to the guillotine.

At last his turn came: Charles Evrémonde, called Darnay, faced the judge and jury. The jurymen sat with the judge (the President); they wore feathered hats. The judgement hall was crowded with both men and women, the roughest, the cruellest, the lowest people of Paris. These people followed every trial very closely. Their loud cries of approval or of disapproval often stopped the work of the court. They greeted every sentence of death with the wildest shouts of joy. The men were armed in various ways and all wore red caps. Even many of the women carried knives; some ate and drank as they looked on; many of them knitted. Among those who knitted was a determined-looking woman who sat next to the man that Darnay recognized as Defarge. From time to time she whispered in his ear: she seemed to be his wife.

Below the President of the court sat Dr Manette, in his dark clothes. The only other person in the court who wore ordinary clothes was Mr Lorry.

Charles Evrémonde, called Darnay, was accused as an émigré; as an émigré he was accused under the law which forbade the return of all émigrés to France. It was of no importance that the law had been passed since his return. He was an émigré and

81

should be sentenced to death.

'Take off his head!' shouted the people watching. 'An enemy of the Republic!'

The President rang the bell to silence these cries. Then he asked the accused, 'Is it true that you have lived for many years in England?'

'Certainly it is true,' answered Darnay.

'Then you are not an émigré?'

'I am not an émigré within the meaning of the law. I gave up the rank of Marquis because I hated it. I went to live in England and earn my own living there because I did not wish to live on the work of the ill-treated people of France. All that was before the name "émigré" was thought of.'

'What proof have you of this?'

He gave the names of two witnesses: Theophile Gabelle and Alexandre Manette.

'You married in England?'

'Yes, but my wife is a Frenchwoman.'

'A citizeness of France? What is her name and family?'

'Her name is Lucie Manette, only daughter of Dr Manette, well-known to all as a friend of the Republic and an old prisoner of the Bastille.'

This answer and the name of Dr Manette had a positive effect on the people. Cries of joy at the mention of the good Doctor filled the hall. People who a few minutes before had looked with hatred at the accused now began to smile at him.

'Why,' asked the President, 'did you return to France when you did? Why did you not return sooner?'

'I did not return to France sooner because I had no means of living in France; but in England I lived by teaching French language and literature. I returned when I did as a result of a letter from a French citizen whose life was in danger because of my absence. I came back to try to save a citizen's life, to bear witness for him at whatever danger to myself. Is that a crime in the eyes of the Republic?'

The crowd shouted, 'No!' and the President rang his bell again. But they continued crying 'No' until they grew tired.

'What is the name of that citizen?' asked the President.

'He is my first witness, Citizen Gabelle. Monsieur Gabelle's letter is no doubt among the papers in front of the President.'

The Doctor had made sure that the letter was there. It was produced and read.

Citizen Gabelle was called.

'Is this your letter, Citizen Gabelle?'

'It is. I was kept for many months in the Abbaye prison without trial. I was set free only after Citizen Evrémonde had been taken.'

Dr Manette was then questioned. His great popularity and his clear answers produced a great effect. 'Citizen Evrémonde, called Darnay, was my first friend in England. He has always been kind and true to me and to my daughter. He was not liked by the government of England. In fact, that government once put him on trial for his life as an enemy of England. Mr Lorry, an Englishman now present in the court, was at that trial and can bear witness to the truth of this.'

After hearing all this, the jury decided that they knew enough, and that they were ready to give their votes if the President was ready to receive them. The President said he was ready.

The jury voted out loud, one after the other. At every vote, the crowd set up a shout. All the votes were for the prisoner, and the President freed him.

There was a great shout of joy in the hall. Tears fell freely, and hundreds crowded round Darnay. It was only with great difficulty that he was freed from them. But these same people would have been just as ready to tear him from his guards and murder him.

As soon as Darnay was taken away, five others took his place. They were to be tried as enemies of the Republic, for they had not supported it by word or action. Their trials did not take long. They were all ordered to be put to death before Darnay had managed to get away from the court.

Many of those who had been present at the trial of Darnay went with him into the street. There they were joined by hundreds of others, all cheering and laughing. But the faces of Defarge and his wife were not among them.

The people forced Darnay into a chair and lifted it on their shoulders. Then, in a wild procession, followed by hundreds of happy citizens, Charles was carried through the streets until he came to the courtyard of the house of Dr Manette. There they put him down and he rushed up the steps to where his wife was waiting. When the people saw him hold out his arms and saw her fall fainting into them, men and women kissed one another with joy, and began dancing in the courtyard. When they had had enough of this, they put a young woman in the chair, lifted her on their shoulders, cried that she was the Goddess of Liberty. Then they left, still cheering and shouting, and went back to the courtroom.

Lucie grew quiet, and both stood looking at each other for a long time.

'Lucie, my own! Safe at last!' said Darnay softly to his wife.

'Dearest Charles! Let us thank God who has brought you safely through so many dangers.'

They lowered their heads and gave their thanks. Little Lucie was held up by Miss Pross to be kissed. She put her arms round her father's neck and did not let go.

Then, breathless, but proud and happy, came Dr Manette, followed shortly afterwards by Mr Lorry. They shook hands warmly with Darnay.

'And now, my dear,' said Darnay to Lucie, 'we must thank

your father. No other man in the whole of France could have done what he has done for me.'

Lucie laid her head on her father's breast without speaking, as she had laid his head on her breast in Paris, long, long ago.

'You must not be weak, my dearest,' he said. 'Do not be afraid. Did I not tell you that I should save him? Well, I have saved him.'

Chapter 19   A Knock at the Door

Although Darnay had been saved, Lucie could not feel completely happy, and her heart was full of fear. The blameless were so often put to death. Many as free of guilt as her husband, many as dear to others as he was to her, every day shared the end from which he had been saved.

Her father felt differently. He had carried out the work that he had set himself and had kept his promise to set Charles free. Having proved his power, he wanted the others to depend on him in this difficult time.

Miss Pross and Jerry Cruncher were getting ready to go out to buy food at the little shops near their rooms. Miss Pross stopped to ask the Doctor a question:

'Is there any hope yet of our leaving this place?'

'I fear not,' he answered. 'It would be dangerous for Charles if he tried to go away.'

'Well, we must have patience and wait,' said Miss Pross. 'Now, Mr Cruncher!'

They went out, leaving Lucie, her husband, her father and her child by a bright fire. Mr Lorry was expected back soon from the bank. All was quiet and Lucie was more relaxed than she had ever been.

'What is that?' she cried suddenly.

'My dear!' said her father, laying his hands on hers. 'Be calm!'

'I thought I heard strange feet on the stairs!'

'My dear, the stairs are perfectly quiet.'

As he said this, a heavy blow was struck on the door.

The Doctor picked up the lamp and went to open it, while Lucie sat waiting in terror. He found outside four rough men in red caps armed with swords and guns.

'The Citizen Evrémonde, called Darnay,' said the first man, as they all walked in.

'Who wants him?' answered Darnay.

'I want him. We want him. I know you, Evrémonde; I saw you in the court today. You are again the prisoner of the Republic.'

The four surrounded him, where he stood with his wife and child holding on to him.

'Tell me why I am again a prisoner.'

'It is enough that you return with us. You will know tomorrow. You will be tried tomorrow.'

Dr Manette seemed turned into stone: he stood with the lamp in his hand as if he were in a dream. After these words were spoken, he put the lamp down and faced the speaker.

'Do you know who I am?' said the Doctor.

'Yes, I know you, Citizen Doctor.'

'Will you answer his question for me, then? How has this happened?'

'Citizen Doctor,' said the first of the men, 'he has been accused by people in the Quarter of Saint-Antoine. This citizen,' he added, pointing to the second of the men who had entered, 'comes from Saint-Antoine.'

The second man moved his head in agreement. 'He is accused by Saint-Antoine.'

'Of what?' asked the Doctor.

'Citizen Doctor,' said the first man, 'ask no more. Evrémonde, we are in a hurry.'

'One moment,' begged the Doctor. 'Will you tell me who accused him?'

'It is against the rules. But – well – he is accused by Citizen and Citizeness Defarge. And by one other.'

'What other?'

'You will be answered tomorrow,' said the man from Saint-Antoine.

Chapter 20   Miss Pross Finds her Brother

Knowing nothing whatever of the events at home, Miss Pross made her way through the narrow streets. She was thinking about the things she had to buy for the family. Mr Cruncher walked at her side, carrying the basket. They looked into all the shops as they passed, but were careful to avoid excited groups of people.

Miss Pross bought some food and some oil for the lamp; then she remembered that she had to buy some wine. She looked into several wine shops, but did not enter because they were crowded and noisy. After a time she found one that was quieter and not quite so crowded. This she entered.

A number of people were inside; most of them armed. Some were playing cards; one was reading a newspaper aloud, and others were listening to him. One or two had fallen asleep in their chairs. Miss Pross and Jerry went up to the shopkeeper and asked for wine.

As the wine was being measured, a man parted from another in a corner and rose to his feet to go out. As he left he had to face Miss Pross. No sooner did he face her, than Miss Pross cried out.

Everybody looked up to see what was happening. They saw

only a man and a woman looking closely at each other: the man had all the appearance of a Frenchman; the woman was clearly English.

'Oh, Solomon, dear Solomon,' cried Miss Pross. 'After not laying eyes on you for so many years, have I found you at last?'

'Don't call me Solomon! Do you want to be the death of me?' asked the man in a frightened and angry manner.

'Brother, brother!' cried Miss Pross. 'How can you ask me such a cruel question?'

'Then hold your tongue,' said Solomon, 'and come outside, if you want to speak to me. Pay for your wine and come out. Who is this man?'

Miss Pross, shaking her head sadly at her unloving brother, said, 'Mr Cruncher.'

'Let him come out, too,' said Solomon. 'Does he think I am a ghost?'

Mr Cruncher looked as if he had seen a ghost, so great was the look of surprise on his face. But he said nothing and followed Miss Pross out of the shop.

As they were going out, Solomon turned to the people and said a few words in French that caused them to continue with what they were doing.

'Now,' said Solomon, stopping at a dark street corner, 'what do you want?'

'How unkind you are to speak to me in such a manner!' said poor Miss Pross.

Solomon bent down his head and gave her one short kiss.

'There! Now are you satisfied?'

Miss Pross shook her head and cried in silence.

'If you expect me to be surprised,' said her brother, 'I'm not. I knew you were here. It is my business to know most of the strangers who are here. If you don't want to put my life in danger, go your way as soon as possible, and let me go mine. I'm busy. I am an official.'

'Just say one loving word to me before you go,' said Miss Pross.

'Wait a minute! Don't go yet,' said Mr Cruncher. 'I want to ask you something. Is your name John Solomon or Solomon John?'

Solomon turned to him with great distrust.

'Come!' said Mr Cruncher. 'Speak out, John Solomon or Solomon John? She calls you Solomon, and she ought to know, being your sister. And I know you are John. Which name comes first? And what about the name of Pross? That wasn't your name in England.'

'What do you mean?'

'I know that Pross wasn't your name, but I can't remember what you called yourself. And the other man, your friend, had a very short name. Now what did you call yourself at that time?'

'Barsad!' said another voice, breaking in.

'That's the name! Barsad!' cried Jerry.

'Yes, Barsad,' said Sydney Carton. He stood with his hands behind his back, quite calm and unexcited. 'Don't be worried, my dear Miss Pross,' continued Sydney. 'I arrived at Mr Lorry's office yesterday evening. We agreed that I should not show myself to the family until all was well, or until I could be useful. I came here to have a little talk with your brother. I wish your brother had better employment. I wish, for you, that he was not a police spy.'

The spy, who was pale, turned paler. 'How do you dare—?'

'I'll tell you,' said Sydney. 'I saw you come out of the Conciergerie an hour or more ago. You have a face that is easily remembered, and I remember faces well. I was surprised to see you coming out of the prison. I remembered that you were connected with Mr Darnay's former misfortune in England; so I followed you. I was just behind you when you entered the wine shop. I sat near you and listened to your conversation and to what others said about you. In this way I discovered the nature of your employment. And gradually I made a decision, Mr Barsad.'

'What decision?'

'It would be difficult, it might be dangerous to talk about it in the street. Will you please come with me for a few minutes to the office of Mr Lorry?'

'What if I refuse to come?'

'I think you had better come. You will be sorry if you don't.'

'This is all your fault,' said the spy, looking angrily at his sister.

'Not at all,' said Sydney. 'Only my great respect for your sister forces me to be so polite to you. Will you come?'

'I'll hear what you have got to say. Yes, I'll come.'

'I suggest that we first take your sister safely to the corner of her own street. Let me take your arm, Miss Pross. Paris is a bad city to be out in, unprotected. And as Jerry seems to know something about Mr Barsad too, I'll invite him to come with me. Are we ready? Come, then!'

As they walked along, Miss Pross looked up at Carton's face and begged him not to do any harm to her brother. She noticed that he had a very determined look, as if he had come to a great decision that changed him completely. They left her at the corner of her street and Carton led the way to Mr Lorry's office, which was within a few minutes' walk. John Barsad (whose real name was Solomon Pross) walked at his side.

Mr Lorry had just finished his dinner and was sitting in front of a cheerful fire, looking into the flames and thinking of his past life. He turned his head when they entered and showed surprise at the sight of a stranger.

'Miss Pross's brother, sir,' said Sydney. 'He calls himself Mr Barsad.'

'Barsad?' repeated the old gentleman. 'Barsad? I seem to know the name and the face.'

'I told you that your face was easily remembered, Mr Barsad,' said Sydney coldly. 'Please sit down.'

As he took a chair himself, he helped Mr Lorry to remember by saying, 'Barsad was a witness at that trial in London.'

Mr Lorry remembered immediately, and gave his new visitor a look of deep dislike.

'Mr Barsad was recognized by Miss Pross as her long-lost, much-loved brother,' said Sydney. 'And he has admitted the relationship. I pass to worse news. Darnay has been taken to prison again!'

'What did you say? I left him safe and free only two hours ago, and was just about to return to him.'

'He has been retaken. When was it done, Mr Barsad?'

'A short time ago.'

'No one knows better than Mr Barsad. I heard him mention it recently in a wine shop. He saw Darnay taken into the Conciergerie. There is no doubt about it.'

Mr Lorry remained silent. He was deeply worried.

'Now,' said Sydney, 'I hope that the name and influence of Dr Manette may be as useful tomorrow as it was today. The trial will be tomorrow, Mr Barsad?'

'I believe so.'

'But this time things may be different. It is a bad sign that the Doctor was unable to prevent them taking him.'

'He may not have known of it,' said Mr Lorry.

'But that, too, would be a bad sign. In short, this is a very dangerous time, and a dangerous game must be played. Let the Doctor play his game and I'll play mine. No man's life here is worth anything. Anyone carried home by the people today may be sent back to prison or to the guillotine tomorrow. Now, if the worst happens, I shall need the help of a friend in the Conciergerie where Darnay will be tried again. I shall use

Mr Barsad's help. It is like a game of cards between him and me. If I win the game of cards, I get his help.'

'You'll need very good cards to win that!' said the spy.

'I'll show you my cards. Mr Lorry, you know my weakness; I wish you'd give me some wine.'

It was put before him. He drank a glass and pushed the bottle away thoughtfully. Then he went on, speaking slowly as if he were a card player looking at the cards which he held in his hand. 'Mr Barsad,' he said, 'you are a police spy, a messenger of the Republican committees, a secret informer – but you are using a false name! That's a good card, a useful card to me. Mr Barsad, now in the service of the Republican government of France, was once in the service of the English government. That's a very useful card to me. Why? Because everyone will think that Mr Barsad is still in the service of the English government, is a spy for them, is an enemy right in the heart of France. That's a card that cannot be beaten. You see my cards, Mr Barsad?'

'How do you plan to play those cards?' said Barsad.

'I play my best card first. I tell the nearest Republican committee that Mr Barsad is an enemy of the Republic, an enemy of France. Look at your cards, Mr Barsad, and see what you have. Don't hurry.'

He drew the bottle nearer, poured out a glassful and drank it.

'Look at your cards carefully, Mr Barsad. Take your time!'

The spy looked at his cards. They were poor ones. There were bad cards that even Sydney Carton knew nothing of. Barsad had been thrown out of his employment in England as a police spy for unsuccessful lying; he had crossed to France to do the same dishonourable work there, for the French government. First he spied on his own countrymen in France; then he spied on Frenchmen. The French royal government had employed him to spy on Saint-Antoine and the Defarges. The royal government had given Barsad information about Dr Manette so that he could get into conversation with the Defarges. He had tried to do so but had failed. He remembered how that terrible woman had knitted as he spoke to her. He had seen her since give information against many people out of her knitted list, and all of them had very soon been sent to the guillotine. He knew that a spy had many enemies and was never safe: and that even the smallest mistake was enough to put an end to a man's life. He held no winning cards, only losing ones.

'You don't seem to like your cards,' said Sydney calmly.

Barsad turned to Mr Lorry. 'I beg you to persuade him not to speak. I admit that I am a spy and that it is considered a dishonourable kind of work. But somebody must do it. Surely the gentleman would not act as a spy and informer himself.'

'Do I get your help, Mr Barsad? Or shall I go to the nearest Republican committee?' He took out his watch. 'You have only a few minutes in which to decide.'

'But, sir, surely your respect for my sister will prevent you from—'

'The best way I can show my respect for your sister is by getting rid of her brother.'

'You think so?'

'I am sure of it.'

The spy remained silent. All his confidence had gone. He felt completely in the other's power.

'Well,' said Sydney, 'I think I have another card. That man you were speaking to in the wine shop, that other spy. I seem to know him. Who was he?'

'A Frenchman,' replied Barsad. 'He is of no importance.'

'Perhaps,' said Sydney. 'I know the face though. He spoke French, but like a foreigner. I'm sure I've seen him before.'

'Impossible,' said the spy.

'I've got him,' cried Sydney, striking the table with his hand, 'Cly! We had that man in front of us at the Old Bailey.'

'You are wrong,' said the spy. 'Cly died in London and was buried.'

Here Mr Cruncher rose to his feet and stepped forward.

'I know something about that,' he said. 'I know that he was not buried. That funeral was not a real one. There was no dead body in the grave. The box contained stones. That funeral was arranged so that everybody would think that he was dead and would stop looking for him.'

'Jerry,' said Mr Lorry, 'how did you, a trusted employee of Tellson's, become involved in such terrible things, and how did you learn that the box contained stones?'

'I can't tell you, sir, at least, not now. But I do know. Look at the man's face. He knows that I am telling the truth. I should like to kill the pair of them.'

Mr Barsad's face had gone very white and his mouth was half open with surprise.

'I see one thing,' said Carton. 'Mr Barsad is the friend of a man about whom there is a mystery, a man who was dead and came to life again. That is a strange thing. Perhaps I shall say that there are two foreign spies, both working in the prisons, both enemies of the Republic. That seems to be another good card. Will you play, Mr Barsad?'

'No,' said Barsad. 'I give up. I admit that the people in London hated Cly and myself so much that we had to escape. I got away with difficulty. And Cly would never have escaped if that false funeral had not been arranged. But it is a mystery to me how this man knows about it.'

'Never mind about that,' said Jerry. 'I do know and that's enough. The next funeral you and Cly attend will be real ones, and your own, I hope.'

The spy turned from him to Sydney Carton.

'What do you want me to do? I go on duty soon and must not be late. Remember, you must not ask too much of me. If you ask me to put myself in great danger, I shall refuse and give information against you. It might be more dangerous for me to agree than to refuse. We are all in danger. What do you want?'

'Not much. You work at the Conciergerie and can get in?'

'I tell you that an escape is impossible.'

'Who spoke of an escape? Do you work at the Conciergerie?'

'I do sometimes.'

'You can go there when you choose?'

'I can pass in and out when I choose.'

Carton filled another glass with wine, changed his mind about drinking it, and poured it slowly out on to the floor.

'Now, Mr Barsad, come with me into the next room, and let us have a last word alone.'

Chapter 21   Sydney Carton Makes his Plans

When Carton and Barsad had gone into the next room, Mr Lorry looked at Jerry with doubt and distrust.

'Jerry,' he said, 'come here.'

Mr Cruncher came forward slowly.

'What have you been, besides a messenger? I believe, Jerry, that you have been using the great bank of Tellson's to hide other, unlawful business. If you have, don't expect me to keep your secret.'

'I hope, sir,' said Jerry, 'that you will never bring harm to a poor man like me. Doctors need bodies for their studies. Somebody has to get them.'

'Ugh!' cried Mr Lorry. 'I can't believe what I am hearing.'

'Sir, don't be too hard on me. I did not need to tell you. I could have kept it back. I only said it in a good cause.'

'That is true,' said Mr Lorry. 'Say no more now. I may still be your friend if you behave better in the future.'

At that moment Sydney Carton and the spy returned. 'Goodbye, Mr Barsad,' said the former. 'Our arrangement is made and you have nothing to fear from me.'

As Barsad left, Mr Lorry asked what Carton had done.

'Not much. I have arranged to reach Darnay in prison, if necessary.'

'That alone will not help him,' said Mr Lorry.

'I never said it would.'

Mr Lorry sat looking into the fire. He was an old man now, filled with sympathy for Lucie and with anxiety for her husband, and his tears fell.

'Don't tell Lucie of this arrangement,' said Carton. 'She might imagine a thousand reasons for it and any of them would only add to her troubles. I had better not see her at all. I can do any little helpful work that my hand can find to do, without that. You are going to see her, I hope. She must be very unhappy tonight.'

'I am going now.'

'I am glad of that. She depends so much on you. How does she look?'

'She has been anxious and unhappy, but very beautiful.'

'Ah!' said Carton slowly. Then after a pause he continued: 'Your duties here have come to an end, sir?'

'Yes. I have done all I can here. I hoped to leave the others in perfect safety. I have got my permission to leave. I was ready to go.'

They were both silent.

'Yours is a long life to look back on, sir?' said Carton.

'I am in my seventy-eighth year.'

'All your life, you have been useful, trusted and respected?'

'I have been busy since I was a boy. But I am not married, and now I am rather lonely. There is nobody to cry for me.'

'Wouldn't Lucie cry for you? And her child?'

'Yes, yes, thank God. I didn't mean what I said.'

'If you had not earned the love and respect of others in your life, if you had done nothing good to be remembered by, your seventy-eight years would be seventy-eight bad memories, would they not?'

'Yes, I think so,' said Mr Lorry.

Carton ended the conversation here by standing up to help Mr Lorry to put on his overcoat.

'I'll walk with you to her gate, Mr Lorry. I will see you in the court tomorrow. Take my arm, sir.'

They went downstairs and out into the streets. When they reached Lucie's gate, Mr Lorry went in. Carton waited a little and then turned back to the gate and touched it.

'She came out here,' he said, 'as she went daily to the prison. She walked often on these stones. Let me follow in her steps.'

It was ten o'clock at night when he stood outside the prison of La Force. He stopped under a lamp and wrote with his pencil on a small piece of paper. Then, going through some dark and dirty streets, he stopped at a shop where medicines were sold. He laid the paper in front of the shopkeeper.

'You will be careful with it, citizen?' said the man as he handed over a small packet. 'You know its effects?'

'Perfectly.'

He put it in his pocket carefully and left the shop.

All night Carton wandered through the streets of the city, but as the sun rose, he fell asleep on the bank of the River Seine. When he awoke, he stood watching the water for a little while and then made his way back to Mr Lorry's rooms. The good old man had already left for the court. Carton drank a little coffee, ate some bread, and then washed and changed his clothes and went out to the court. Mr Lorry was there. Dr Manette was there. Lucie was there, sitting beside her father.

When her husband was brought in, she gave him such an encouraging look, so full of love and gentleness, that it brought the blood into his face and brightened his eyes. In that unjust court, there was little order and no accused person could be sure of a fair trial. It was clear from the strict expressions on the faces of the five judges and of the jury that no mercy could be expected from them that day.

The main points of the case were read out to the court.

'Charles Evrémonde, called Darnay. Set free yesterday. Reaccused and brought back yesterday. Accused as an enemy of the Republic, an aristocrat, member of a family guilty of terrible cruelty to the people.'

'Is he accused openly or secretly?' asked the President.

'Openly, Monsieur President.'

'By whom?'

'By three. Ernest Defarge, Thérèse Defarge, his wife, and Alexandre Manette, doctor.'

A roar rose in the court, in the middle of which Dr Manette was seen, pale and shaking, standing where he had been seated.

'President, I tell you that this is false. You know the accused to be the husband of my daughter. Who says that I accuse the husband of my child?'

'Citizen Manette, be calm. Listen to what is to follow. Right now, be silent!'

Loud cheers again broke out as the Doctor sat down, his lips trembling.

When the court was quiet again, Defarge stood up and described the story of Dr Manette's time in prison and the state of the prisoner when he was set free and delivered to him.

'You did good service at the taking of the Bastille, Citizen Defarge?'

'I believe so.'

'Tell us what you did on that day, citizen.'

'I knew,' said Defarge, looking down at his wife, 'I knew that the prisoner had been kept in a room called One Hundred and Five, North Tower. I learned it from his own lips. He knew himself by no other name than One Hundred and Five, North Tower. When the Bastille fell, I went to that cell, led by one of the guards. I examined the room very carefully. In a hole in the chimney, I found a written paper. This is that written paper. It is in the handwriting of Dr Manette. I pass this paper, in the handwriting of Dr Manette, to the President.'

'Let it be read!'

In the dead silence the paper was read.

Chapter 22   The Doctor's Story

I, Alexandre Manette, am writing this in the Bastille Prison in the year 1767. I intend to hide it in a hole in the chimney where someone may find it after I am dead. I am in my right mind now. I am not crazy (though I fear that very soon I may become so). What I am writing is the truth; I am writing it with an old nail for a pen, and for ink I am using my own blood mixed with dirt from the chimney.

I was walking by the River Seine one cloudy, moonlit night in December 1757. A carriage drove up, behind me. As it came near a head was put out of the window and a man ordered the carriage to stop. Then the voice called me by name. Two gentlemen got out; I noticed that they were very much like one another in height, manner, voice and face.

'You are Dr Manette?' said one of them.

'Gentlemen,' I replied, 'I am.'

'We have been to your house,' they said, 'and were told where we might find you. Please get into the carriage.'

I answered: 'I usually ask what is the nature of the case to which I am called, and the name of those who ask my help.'

'We are men of good family, and as to the nature of the case, you will see that for yourself,' they said, standing one on each side of me. So I had to get in.

The carriage went out from the north gate, left the main road about 2 miles beyond it and came to a lonely house.

I heard cries coming from an upper room. I was taken there and found a young woman in high fever, her mind wandering. She was very beautiful and quite young. Her hair was wild, and her arms were tied to her side by a silk cloth. On a corner of the cloth was the letter E. Her eyes were wild and she kept crying out, 'My husband, my father, and my brother!' and then counted, 'One, two, three...' up to twelve. Then she seemed to listen. Then she began again, over and over.

'How long has she been like this?' I asked.

'Since about this time last night,' said the older of the two brothers.

I gave the girl some medicine to send her to sleep and sat down by the bed to watch the effect. After about half an hour she became quieter. The older brother then said, 'There is another.' He took up a lamp and led me to another room – a place used for keeping food for the horses and firewood. The horses were below.

Lying on the floor was a boy aged about seventeen. His right hand was holding his breast. His eyes were wild. I could see at once that he was dying. When he let me take his hand away, I saw that there was a long deep cut from a sword, made about 24 hours earlier.

'How did this happen?' I asked.

'He is just a village boy; he forced my brother to draw his sword.' There was no pity or sorrow in his voice.

The boy's eyes turned to me. 'She – have you seen her, Doctor?' he asked.

'I have seen her.'

'She is my sister. She loved a young man in the village. He was ill at the time and my sister married him so that she could take care of him. Then the younger of the brothers saw her – and wanted her. They made the man work all night; in the morning they made him pull a cart. One day at midday, just as the clock struck 12, he gave a cry – a cry for each stroke of the clock; then he died. They took her away. When my father heard about it he died of grief. I took my other younger sister away to a place of safety. Then I followed the brother here. Last night I climbed into the house with a sword in my hand. My sister heard me and ran in. Then he came. I struck at him with my sword so that he was forced to draw his sword to save his life. And this is the result. Lift me up, Doctor. Where is he?'

I lifted him, and suddenly, with all his remaining strength, he stood up.

'Marquis,' he said, 'I call on you and yours, the last of a bad race, to pay for these things. I make this cross of blood on you as a sign. And I call on your brother, the worst of a bad race, to pay. I make this cross of blood on him as a sign.'

Twice he put his hand to the cut in his breast and made a cross in the air. Then his hand fell. As I laid him down, I knew he was dead.

I went back to the young woman. She was still crying out. I knew that this would last for some hours and end only in death.

The older brother came and sat near me.

'Doctor,' he said, 'you are a young man and have your future to consider. It would be better for you not to say anything about what you have seen and heard here.'

I did not answer.

The girl died two hours later. The brothers were sitting downstairs. The older brother took a bag of gold from his pocket and offered it to me.

'Please excuse me,' I said. 'I do not want your money.'

They looked at each other and we parted without another word.

Early next morning the bag of gold was left at my house. I had decided to write to the Minister telling him about this matter. Just as I had finished my letter I was told that a young lady wished to see me. In some way she had discovered the main facts of the story. Her husband was the younger brother, but she was not happy in her marriage. She did not know that the girl was dead but hoped to help in some way, secretly. She knew of the younger sister of the dead girl and hoped to help her too. I told her all I knew, and said that I did not know where the younger sister was. When I went with her to the door I saw in her carriage a boy aged about three.

'For my child, Doctor,' she said, 'I want to do all I can for this cruelly wronged family. If I do not, this will be with him all his life. I have a feeling that he may be forced to pay for these wrongs one day, if nothing is done. I have some jewels: I shall order him on my deathbed to give them to this family which his father has wronged.'

She kissed the boy and said, 'You will be true, little Charles?'

The child answered bravely, 'Yes.'

She had mentioned her husband's name, thinking that I knew it, but I made no change in the letter. I closed it and delivered it myself that day.

That night, a man dressed in black rang the bell and demanded to see me. My servant, a youth named Ernest Defarge, opened the door. The stranger followed Defarge upstairs to where I was sitting with my dear wife.

'There is an urgent case in the rue Saint-Honoré,' said the man. 'I have a carriage waiting.'

As soon as I was outside the house a black cloth was thrown over my mouth from behind and my arms were tied. The two brothers came out of the darkness on the other side of the road. The older brother (the Marquis) took from his pocket the letter which I had written to the Minister, burned it in the flame of the carriage lamp and ground the ashes into the mud. Not a word was said. Then the carriage brought me to this prison, to my living grave.

In all these years, these men have sent me no news of my wife. I do not know if she is alive or dead. There is no mercy in their hearts, and God will show them no mercy. The mark of the red cross will be a curse on them forever.

And I, Alexandre Manette, lay my curse on the two brothers and on their children and grandchildren to the last of their evil race.

♦

A terrible sound rose up from the people in the court when the reading of this paper was finished – a cry for blood.

There was no need now to ask why the Defarges had kept the paper secret. They had kept it until the time when it would have its greatest effect. There was no need now to ask why the people of Saint-Antoine hated the Evrémonde family with an undying hatred.

'The Doctor has much influence around him, has he?' whispered Madame Defarge, with a smile to the woman called The Revenge, who was sitting next to her. 'Save him, my Doctor, save him if you can.'

At every juryman's vote there was a roar. Another and another. Roar and roar.

All agreed! Evrémonde, called Darnay, must go back to the prison and to the guillotine within 24 hours!

Chapter 23   Mr Lorry Gives a Promise

Lucie stretched out her arms to her husband.

'Let me touch him once! Let me kiss him! Oh, good citizens, have pity on us!'

Most of the "good citizens" had gone outside to shout their hatred against the prisoner. Among those left in the courtroom was Barsad.

'Let her kiss her husband,' he said. 'It is only for a moment.'

They silently agreed, and she went to where Charles was standing. Her father followed her and would have fallen on his knees to both of them, but Darnay seized him, crying:

'No, no! What have you done that you should kneel to us? We know now what you suffered when you knew who I was. We know how you put Lucie's feelings before your own. We thank you with all our hearts. God be with you!'

As he was taken away, his wife stood looking after him, with her hands pressed together and a look of love on her face. As he disappeared, she turned and fell at her father's feet.

Then, coming from the dark corner where he had been waiting, Sydney Carton picked her up and carried her to the carriage. When they arrived home, he carried her into the house, where her child and Miss Pross cried over her.

'Before I go,' said Carton, 'may I kiss her?' He bent down and touched her face with his lips, and then went into the next room followed by Mr Lorry and the Doctor.

'You had great influence yesterday, Dr Manette,' said Carton. 'You must do your best between now and tomorrow afternoon to save him.'

'I intend to try. I will not rest for a moment.'

'Good. There is little hope and I expect nothing. But I should like to know how you get on. When will you have seen those who are in power?'

'In an hour or two.'

'If I go to Mr Lorry's at nine, shall I hear what you have done?'

'Yes.'

'Good luck!'

Mr Lorry followed Carton to the outer door. He touched Sydney on the shoulder and caused him to turn.

'I have no hope,' said Mr Lorry in a sorrowful voice.

'Nor have I.'

'After the way in which the people showed their feelings, no one would dare let him go.'

'Yes, he will die. There is no real hope,' answered Carton, and walked with a determined step down the stairs.

In the street he paused, not quite decided where to go. 'I shall do well,' he thought, 'to show myself. It is a good idea that these people should know there is a man like me here. It may be a necessary preparation.' And he turned his face towards Saint-Antoine.

He had his dinner, and for the first time in many years he had no strong drink with it. Then he went to the wine shop of Monsieur Defarge. As he walked in, took his seat and asked (in bad French) for a small amount of wine, Madame Defarge took a careless look at him and then a sharper look, and then a sharper.

Madame Defarge walked up to Carton himself and asked what he had ordered.

He repeated what he had already said.

'English?' asked Madame.

'Yes, Madame, I am English.'

She left him to get the wine and said to her husband, 'I swear to you, he is very like Evrémonde!'

'Certainly, he is a little like.'

'Evrémonde is so much in your mind,' said Jacques Three, who was standing near.

A silence fell on them as they looked at Carton, who was pretending to read a paper with difficulty, following the words with his finger.

'What Madame says is true,' said Jacques Three. 'Why stop at Evrémonde?'

'One must stop somewhere,' said Defarge.

'I shall stop when they are all dead,' said Madame.

'A good idea,' said Defarge, rather troubled. 'But the Doctor has suffered greatly. You saw his face when the paper was read. And you saw his daughter.'

'I saw his face. And I saw his daughter,' said Madame Defarge. 'I have seen her today and on other days. I have seen her in the street by the prison. Let her take care. But you – you would save this man even now, if you could.'

'No,' said Defarge.

'Listen,' said Madame. 'This family has long been on my list for their cruelty. When my husband brought home the paper which he found in the Bastille, we read it here, by the light of this lamp. When we had finished it, I told him a secret. That family, treated so badly by the Evrémonde brothers, was my family. That boy they killed was my brother. His sister was my sister.'

'It is true,' said Defarge.

'Then tell others where to stop, but don't tell me!'

Other people entered the shop and the group was broken up. The Englishman paid for his wine and went on his way.

When he arrived at Mr Lorry's room again, he found the old gentleman walking up and down in restless anxiety. Dr Manette had not been seen since he left the bank at four o'clock. They waited until ten o'clock, but he did not come; then Mr Lorry went to Lucie, and Carton sat down by the fire, alone in Mr Lorry's room.

At about 12 o'clock Mr Lorry returned; soon afterwards they heard the Doctor's feet on the stairs. As soon as he entered the room, it was plain that all was lost.

Whether he had really been to anyone, or whether he had been all that time walking the streets, was never known. They asked him no questions, for his face told them everything.

'I cannot find it,' he said. 'Where is it? Where is my bench?'

They looked at one another, and their hearts died within them.

'Come, come,' cried the Doctor. 'Let me get to work.'

It was so clearly useless to reason with him that they each put a hand on his shoulder and persuaded him to sit down by the fire, with a promise that he would soon have his work. He sank into the chair and looked into the fire with tears in his eyes.

Again they looked at one another.

'The last chance is gone,' said Carton. 'He had better be taken to her. But will you listen to me for a moment? Don't ask why I demand a promise from you. I have a good reason.'

'I do not doubt it,' said Mr Lorry. 'Go on.'

Carton bent down to pick up the Doctor's coat, which had fallen to the floor. As he did so, a small case fell out of the Doctor's pocket. Carton took it up. There was a folded paper in it. He opened it, and cried, 'Thank God.'

'What is it?' asked Mr Lorry.

'One moment! Let me speak of it in its place. First,' – he put his hand in his coat and took another paper from it – 'this is the paper which will let me pass out of this city. Look at it. You see – Sydney Carton, an Englishman?'

Mr Lorry held it in his hand, watching Carton's face.

'Keep it for me until tomorrow. I shall see Charles tomorrow, you remember, and I had better not take it into the prison. Now take this paper that Dr Manette had carried about with him: it will let him and his daughter and her child leave the city at any time, you see.'

'Yes.'

'Now listen,' said Carton. 'I have reason to believe that this paper may be taken away from Dr Manette. They are in great danger. I heard Madame Defarge talking about them tonight. Don't look so frightened. You will save them all.'

'I hope I may. But how?'

'I am going to tell you how. It will depend on you, and it could depend on no better man. They are probably safe for a few days.'

'Yes.'

'You have money and can buy the means of travelling to the coast quickly. Early tomorrow arrange to have your horses ready to start at two o'clock tomorrow afternoon.'

'It will be done!'

'You have a good heart. Tell her tonight what you know of the danger to herself, her father and her child. Tell her she must leave Paris. Tell her that it was her husband's last wish. Tell her that more depends on it than she dare believe or hope. Have all the arrangements made in the courtyard here. Even take your place in the carriage. Wait for nothing but to have my place occupied. Then, take the road for England!'

'I understand that I must wait for you at all costs?'

'You have my paper in your hand with the rest. Only wait to have my place occupied.'

'Then I shall have a young man at my side?'

'Yes, you will! Promise me that you will follow my advice exactly.'

'I promise!'

'Do your part, and I will do mine! Now, goodbye!'

Carton helped Mr Lorry to take the Doctor to his daughter. He left them at the gate and remained there for a few minutes alone, looking up at the light in the window of Lucie's room: before he went away, he breathed a last prayer towards it.

Chapter 24   The Great Escape

Charles Darnay, alone in his prison, had no hope. After listening to the reading of the Doctor's paper and hearing the shouts of the crowd, he knew that no personal influence could possibly save him. He knew that he must die, not for any crime of his own, but for all the crimes against millions of common people that members of his own and of other aristocratic families were guilty of.

But it was hard to die, hard to leave again, and for ever, the wife and child whom he had held in his arms after so long a separation. It was some comfort to remember that there was no shame in the end that he must meet; many others who had carried out no crime went along the same road every day and followed it firmly to the end. So when he had become calm, he sat down to write his last letter to those he loved.

He wrote to Lucie:

. . . I never knew that your father was in prison, until you told me of it. I did not know that it was my own uncle and my father who had wronged him cruelly. I told your father my real name, Evrémonde; and he asked me not to tell you what it was, but he allowed the marriage. No doubt he thought that the paper hidden in the Bastille was destroyed when the Bastille was taken – or perhaps he had forgotten it. Comfort your father. Do not let him blame himself in any way. Forget your sorrow and give your life to him and to the care of our child. Some day, in that happier world beyond death, we shall all meet again.

He wrote another letter to the Doctor himself, giving his wife and child into his care and urging him to look after them. This, he thought, might prevent the Doctor from losing his mind again.

The last letter he wrote was to Mr Lorry, explaining all his worldly affairs and thanking him for his lasting friendship. He never thought of Sydney Carton at all; his mind was so full of the others that he never gave him a single thought.

Charles Darnay finished these letters before the lights were put out. When the room became dark, he lay down and thought that he had finished with the world. But the world, the bright world that he had loved, came back to him in his troubled sleep. He dreamed he was back in the house at Soho, in London, free and happy, and Lucie was telling him that he had had a bad dream and had never left her. Then he lay awake for a while, then half awake and half asleep, and the long hours dragged slowly by.

Finally, as the first light of morning came and the shadows left his mind, he realized that the last day of his life had come. He and 51 others would never see another morning.

He knew how he would die, but he had never seen the machine that would put an end to his life. He began to think about it, what it would be like, which way his face would be turned, and whether he would be one of the first or one of the last. These and many other thoughts came into his mind as the morning hours rolled slowly by.

He walked up and down and the clocks struck the numbers that he would never hear again. Nine gone for ever; ten gone for ever; eleven gone for ever.

His mind was now at peace. He softly repeated the names of his loved ones and prayed for them. Twelve gone for ever.

He had been told that the last hour was three, but he knew that they would come for him some time before then, since the carts took a long time to move heavily through the streets. He decided that he had only about two more hours to wait, and set himself to strengthen his mind so that later he might be able to strengthen the minds of the others on the journey through the streets.

Calmly, with his arms folded on his breast, he walked up and down. He heard the clocks strike one without surprise. Thanking Heaven for his peace of mind, he thought, 'Only one more hour to wait,' and turned to walk again.

He stopped. He heard footsteps outside his door. The key was put in the lock and turned. As the door was opened, a man said in a low voice, 'He has never seen me here; I have kept out of his way. Go in alone. I will wait here. Lose no time.'

Then the door was opened quickly and closed, and there before him, face to face, a bright smile on his lips, and one finger raised, stood Sydney Carton.

There was something so bright and strange about Sydney that for a moment Charles thought that he was seeing a ghost. But he spoke, and it was Carton's voice: the hand that took his was really Carton's.

'Of all the people on earth, you didn't expect to see me here, did you?' said Carton.

'I could not believe it to be you. I can hardly believe it now. You are not a prisoner?' he asked anxiously.

'No. By accident I possess some power over one of the officers here, and by reason of that power I stand before you. I come from her – your wife; dear Darnay.'

The prisoner took his hand. Carton continued:

'I bring a most urgent request from her. She begs you, as you love her, to do exactly as I say. You are not to ask me questions; I have no time to answer them. You must just do as I say: she orders it. Take off those boots you are wearing and put on these of mine.'

There was a chair against the wall of the cell, behind the prisoner. Moving forward, Carton, with the speed of lightning, got him down on it and stood over him.

'Now put on these. Quick.'

'Carton, there is no escape from this place. It has never been done. It is crazy to try to escape from here.'

'Am I asking you to escape? When I ask you to pass that door, say it is crazy and remain here. Off with that coat. Put on this coat of mine.'

Darnay was like a child in Sydney's hands. Sydney had the determination, the will: Charles was confused and hardly knew whether he was asleep or awake.

'But, Carton, dear Carton! I don't understand.'

'I don't want you to understand. This is what your wife wants. You must do as she says. It is her last request.'

'You are doing no good. You will only add your own death to mine. There is no escape.'

'Have I asked you, my dear Darnay, to pass the door? When I ask that, refuse. There are pen and paper on the table. Is your hand steady enough to write?'

'It was, before you came in.'

'Steady your hand again, and write what I say. Quick, friend, quick! Do as I say.'

Pressing his hand to his head, Darnay sat down at the table. Carton, with his right hand on his breast, stood over him.

'Write exactly as I speak.'

'Who do I address it to?'

'To no one. Just write what I say.'

The prisoner took up the pen and prepared to write.

'"You remember..."' said Carton. 'Write "You remember... the words that passed between us long ago. It is not in your nature to forget them."'

Carton was holding something in his hand; his hand was moving slowly down as he spoke.

'Have you written "forget them"?'

'I have. What is that in your hand? A weapon?'

'No. I am not armed.'

'Then what is it?'

'You will know in a moment. Write on: "I am thankful that the time has come when I can prove my words. That I do so is no cause for sorrow."'

As he spoke these words, his hand moved slowly and softly down to the writer's face.

The pen dropped from Darnay's fingers, and he looked around him in an uncertain manner.

'What smell is that?'

'Smell? I smell nothing. There is nothing here. Take up your pen and finish. Hurry, hurry!'

The prisoner again took up the pen. He seemed to have some difficulty in fixing his attention. He looked at Carton with clouded eyes, but bent once more over the paper.

Carton repeated, "for sorrow". His hand was stealing down again, slowly, silently. He looked at the pen, and saw that it was making meaningless marks on the paper.

The pen fell from Darnay's hand. He tried to stand up, but he had no control over his legs. Carton caught him quickly around the waist and, with his other hand, pressed the cloth over his nose and mouth. For a few seconds Darnay fought against the man who had come to give his life for him: then he lay senseless on the ground.

Quickly, but calmly, Carton dressed himself in the clothes the prisoner had laid on the floor. Then he softly called. 'You can come in now. Come in.'

Barsad, the spy, presented himself.

'You see?' said Carton. 'Is your danger very great?'

Carton knelt down by his friend and put the written paper inside the coat where it would be found.

'Mr Carton,' said the spy anxiously, 'my danger will not be great if you are true to your word.'

'Don't fear me. I will be true to the death.'

'You must be, Mr Carton, if the number is to be right. Fifty-two must die today. If you, in that dress, make the number right, I shall have no fear.'

'Have no fear! I shall soon be out of the way of harming you, or anyone else; and the others, may it please God, will soon be far away from here. Now, call help, and carry me to the carriage.'

'You?' asked the spy.

'Him, of course, with whom I have exchanged. You can go out by the gate by which you brought me in?'

'Of course.'

'I was weak and faint when you brought me in. The last meeting with my friend was too much for me. Such things have often happened before. It isn't the first time that a friend has fainted while trying to say a last goodbye, is it? Your life is in your own hands. Quick! Call for help!'

'You swear to keep our secret?'

'Man, man! Have I not sworn it already? Why do you waste time when there is so little? Take him yourself to the courtyard you know of, place him in the carriage, show him to Mr Lorry and tell him to give him nothing but fresh air. Tell Mr Lorry to remember my words of last night, and to remember his own promise, and to drive away.'

The spy Barsad went out. Carton seated himself at the table, resting his head in his hands. The spy returned immediately, with two men.

'Hello!' said one of the men, looking at the fallen figure. 'Saying his last goodbyes has been too much for him, has it? He didn't like the idea of his friend saying good day to the guillotine.'

They raised the unconscious man between them and moved to the door.

'The time is short, Evrémonde,' said the spy in a warning voice.

'I know it well,' answered Carton. 'Be careful with my friend,

I beg you, and leave me alone.'

'Come then,' said Barsad.'Let us leave him.'

The door closed, the key was turned in the lock and Carton was alone. He listened for any sound that might show that they had been discovered, but nothing happened beyond the usual noises of a prison. He began to breathe more freely, but still listened until the clock struck two.

Then there were sounds, sounds whose meaning he understood: he was ready for them. Several doors were opened one after another, and then his own. A prison guard, with a list in his hand, looked in and said, 'Follow me, Evrémonde.' Sydney got up and followed him until he came to a large, dark room. It was half filled with people, brought there to have their arms tied. Some were standing; some were seated; some were crying, and a few were walking restlessly about. But most of them were silent and still, their eyes lowered.

Sydney stood by the wall in a dark corner. One man stopped in passing as if to greet him, but then went on. A few moments later, a young woman rose from the place where she had been sitting and came to speak to him. She had a slight girlish form, and a sweet thin face in which there was no sign of colour.

'Citizen Evrémonde,' she said, touching him with her cold hand, 'I am a poor little dressmaker who was with you in La Force.'

'True,' he replied.'I forget what you were accused of?'

'Spying. But Heaven knows that I am not guilty. Who would think a poor, weak creature like me was a spy?'

She smiled so sadly as she spoke that tears came into Sydney's eyes.

'I am not afraid to die, for I have done nothing wrong. If the Republic, which is going to do so much good to the poor, will profit by my death, I am ready to die. But how can my death be of use? Such a poor, weak creature!'

Great pity filled Sydney's heart as he looked at her and listened to her. She was the last person that he would ever speak to.

'I heard that you were set free, Citizen Evrémonde. I hoped it was true.'

'It was. But I was taken again.'

'If they let us ride together, Citizen Evrémonde, will you let me hold your hand? I am not afraid, but I am small and weak, and it will give me courage.'

As she lifted her patient eyes to his, he saw a sudden doubt in them, and then surprise. He pressed her work-worn, hunger-worn hands and touched them with his lips.

'Are you dying for him?' she whispered.

'Hush! Yes. And for his wife and child.'

'Oh, will you let me hold your hand, brave stranger?'

'Hush! Yes, my poor sister; to the last.'

Chapter 25   The Last of Paris

Shadows were falling on the gates of the prison. Shadows were falling on the gates of the city. A carriage, going out of Paris, drove up to the gate to be examined.

'Who goes there? Your papers!'

The papers were handed out and read.

'Alexandre Manette. Doctor. French. Which is he?'

'This is he; this weak and helpless old man is he.'

'It seems that the Doctor is not in his right mind. Perhaps the Revolution fever has been more than he can bear?'

'Much more than he can bear.'

'Ha! Many suffer from it! Lucie, his daughter. French. Which is she?'

'This is she.'

'Lucie, the wife of Evrémonde, is it not?'

'It is.'

'Ha! Evrémonde has an appointment elsewhere! Little Lucie, her child, English. This is she?'

'Yes.'

'Kiss me, child of Evrémonde. Now you have kissed a good citizen of the Republic. Something new in the family! Sydney Carton, lawyer, English. Which is he?'

'He lies there.'

'Has he fainted?'

'We hope he will improve in the fresh air. He has just separated sadly from a friend who is on his way to the guillotine.'

'Is that all? That is not much! There are many like that. Jarvis Lorry. Banker. English. Which is he?'

'I am he. Necessarily, being the last.'

It was Jarvis Lorry who replied to all the questions. He was standing by the door of the carriage talking to a group of officials. They slowly examined the carriage and the luggage on its roof.

'Here are your papers, Jarvis Lorry, signed.'

'May we leave, citizen?'

'You may go. Forward! A good journey!'

The first danger was past.

There was fear in the carriage. There was crying, and the heavy breathing of the traveller in the corner.

'Can we not go faster?' asked Lucie.

'It would look as if we were running away,' replied Mr Lorry. 'So far, no one is following us.'

Soon they were out of the city, and in the country. They passed groups of small houses in twos and threes. They went through avenues of leafless trees, past farms and ruined buildings. The horses were changed. They went through a village, up the hill and down the hill and along the low wet ground. Suddenly there was a cry.

'Ho! You, in the carriage there! Speak!'

'What is it?' asked Mr Lorry, looking out of the window.

'How many today?'

'I do not understand you.'

'How many for the guillotine today?'

'Fifty-two.'

'I said so! A good number. My friend here thought it was 42. Ten more heads! I love it! I love the guillotine!'

The night fell. The traveller in the corner began to come to himself and to speak. 'Look out, look out, and see if we are followed!'

The wind was rushing after them and the clouds were flying after them. But, so far, they were followed by nothing else!

Chapter 26   The Knitting Is Finished

A little earlier, while the 52 men and women were spending their last hours on earth, Madame Defarge was talking to her friend, The Revenge, and Jacques Three in the woodcutter's hut. Jacques Three was a member of the jury. The woodcutter (who had once been a roadmender) sat a little apart from the others.

'But our Defarge,' said Jacques Three, 'is surely a good Republican, isn't he?'

'There is none better in France,' cried The Revenge.

'Quiet, little Revenge,' said Madame Defarge. 'My husband is certainly a good Republican and a brave man. He has deserved the Republic's thanks. But he has one weakness. His weakness is that he is sorry for the Doctor.'

'It is a great pity,' said Jacques Three. 'A good Republican should not be sorry for such people.'

'Listen,' said Madame Defarge. 'I care nothing about this

Doctor. He may keep his head or lose it – it is all the same to me. But the Evrémonde family must be destroyed. The wife and child must follow the father.'

'She had a fine head for the guillotine,' remarked Jacques Three. 'I have seen blue eyes and fair hair there, and they looked beautiful when held up and shown to the people.'

Madame Defarge looked down and was lost in thought.

'The child, too,' remarked Jacques Three, enjoying the sound of his own voice, 'has golden hair and blue eyes. We don't often have a child there. It will be a pretty sight.'

Madame Defarge lifted her head. She had come to a decision.

'The truth is that I have lost confidence in my husband. I cannot trust him in this matter. I dare not tell him the details of my plan. I fear that if I delay, he may give them warning and they may escape.'

'That must never be,' said Jacques Three. 'No one must escape. We have not enough heads as it is. We ought to have at least a hundred a day.'

'In a word,' went on Madame Defarge, 'my husband has not the same reason as I have for hunting this family until not one remains alive. And I have not the same reason to feel sorry for the Doctor as he has. I must act for myself, therefore. Come here, little citizen!'

The woodcutter had great respect for Madame Defarge and feared her. He came forward with his hand to his red cap.

'Those signals that she made to the prisoners – are you ready to give evidence about them this very day?'

'Yes, certainly. Why not?' he cried. 'Every day, in all weathers, from two to four o'clock, she was always there. Sometimes she was with the child and sometimes without. I saw her myself.'

'Some secret plan, of course,' said Jacques Three.

'You are sure of the other members of the jury?' asked Madame Defarge.

'You can depend on them, dear citizeness. I can answer for them all.'

'Now let me see,' said Madame Defarge thoughtfully. 'Can I let this Doctor live because of my husband? I have no feeling either way. Can I let him live?'

'He would count as one head,' said Jacques Three. 'We really have not enough heads. It would be a pity, I think.'

'He was signalling with her when I saw them,' she went on. 'I cannot speak about one without the other. No! He must take his chance. I cannot let him live. You are going at three o'clock to see these 52 people guillotined. And I, too, shall be there. After it is all over, come with me. We will go to Saint-Antoine and give information against them together.'

The little woodcutter said that he would be proud and happy to go with Madame Defarge. She looked at him coldly, and, like a nervous dog, he avoided her eyes and went back to his seat.

Madame Defarge waved the others nearer to the door and told them of her plans.

'Lucie Manette will be at home now, waiting for the moment of her husband's death. She will be upset and crying. She will be in such a state of mind that she will say bad things about the justice of the Republic. She will be full of kindness to its enemies. I will go for her!'

'What a woman! A true Republican. Ah! my dear!' cried The Revenge, and kissed her.

'Please take my knitting,' said Madame Defarge, placing it in the hands of The Revenge, 'and have it ready for me in my usual seat. Keep my usual chair for me. Go now – there will be a big crowd.'

'I am happy to do what my chief orders,' said The Revenge, kissing her on the cheek. 'You will not be late?'

'I shall be there before they begin.'

'Be there before the carts arrive. Be sure that you are there, my dear,' said The Revenge, calling after her, since she had already turned into the street, 'before the carts arrive.'

Madame Defarge waved her hand to show that she had heard and would be there in good time. Then she started out with determination through the streets. Of all the women of Paris, there was no one to be more feared than Madame Defarge. She had a strong, fearless character, and a kind of beauty that called attention to her qualities. She had grown up with a deep sense of wrong and a powerful hatred of the aristocracy; any pity that she once may have had was now dead. It was nothing to her that a man without guilt was going to die for the evil actions of others. It was nothing to her that a wife was going to lose her husband, and a child its father. That was not enough. Hidden in the front of her dress was a loaded gun. Hidden at her waist was a sharpened knife. Madame Defarge walked firmly through the streets towards the house of her enemies, dressed like this.

At that very moment, a carriage was just setting out for the north road block. In the carriage was an old Englishman, a young mother and her child, an old Frenchman who seemed to be out of his mind, and a younger man who was lying unconscious.

The question of what to do with Miss Pross and Jerry Cruncher had caused Mr Lorry some worry. He did not want to overload the carriage: the lighter it was, the faster it would travel. And also, the fewer the passengers, the shorter their examination at the road blocks. As every moment was important and might mean the difference between life and death, he decided that Miss Pross and Jerry should travel separately, in a lighter carriage. They should start after the others, but would soon catch up with them and go on ahead to order fresh horses at every town. In this way much valuable time might be saved.

Miss Pross and Jerry had seen the carriage start and had guessed who the unconscious man was whom Barsad had brought. As Madame Defarge was coming nearer to the house, these two, in the greatest anxiety, were discussing what to do.

'Mr Cruncher,' said Miss Pross, 'don't you think it would be a good idea if we did not start from this courtyard? One carriage has already gone from here: another might cause people to talk.'

'I think you are right, Miss,' said Jerry. 'As always, I'm ready to be guided by you.'

'I am in such a state of anxiety that I can hardly think; but suppose you go and tell the people to bring our carriage to another place? I will be waiting for you and you can pick me up.'

'Where shall I find you?'

'At the church of Notre-Dame. You can't make a mistake about that. I'll be waiting for you there. Go along quickly. Be there with the carriage at three o'clock.'

Jerry did not like leaving Miss Pross by herself, and said so.

'Do not think of yourself,' she answered. 'Think of others. I shall be quite safe. In about half an hour we shall be in the carriage together.'

As soon as Jerry had gone, Miss Pross began to get ready for the journey. She got a bowl of water and began to wash her face, because her eyes were red and swollen with recent tears. She did not want to attract any attention as she went through the streets.

As she washed, Miss Pross kept looking behind her to see that nobody was in the room; she felt lonely and afraid at being left alone. Then, as she looked behind, she cried out: she saw a figure standing in the middle of the room.

The bowl fell to the ground, broken, and the water flowed across the floor to the feet of Madame Defarge.

Madame Defarge looked at her coldly, and said, 'The wife of Evrémonde – where is she?'

Miss Pross suddenly realized that the doors of all the rooms were open. Her first act was to shut them. She then placed herself in front of the door of the room that Lucie had occupied.

Madame Defarge watched her doing this and looked angrily

at her when she had finished. Miss Pross returned her look with steady eyes. Both were determined women in their different ways. Hatred had made the heart of the Frenchwoman hard; love now filled the Englishwoman's with courage.

'Although you look like the wife of the devil himself,' said Miss Pross softly, 'you will not get the better of me. I am an Englishwoman.'

Madame Defarge knew well that this woman was a trusted friend of the family. Miss Pross knew that the other woman was the family's enemy.

'I am on my way to a certain place where my seat and my knitting are being kept for me,' said Madame Defarge. 'I wish to see the wife of Evrémonde.'

'I know that your intentions are evil,' said Miss Pross.

Each woman spoke in her own language and neither understood a word of what the other said. But each knew very well the other's intention.

'It will do her no good to keep herself hidden from me,' said Madame Defarge. 'Good patriots will know what that means. Let me see her. Go and tell her I wish to see her. Do you hear?'

'I take no orders from you,' said Miss Pross. 'You evil foreign woman.'

'You pig!' cried Madame Defarge. 'I demand to see her. Either tell her so, or stand out of the way and let me go to her myself.'

Each looked steadily into the other's eyes. Madame Defarge took one step forward.

'I am an Englishwoman,' said Miss Pross. 'I don't care what happens to me. I know that the longer I keep you here, the greater hope there is for my dearest one. If you lay a finger on me, I will not leave a handful of that black hair on your head.'

Miss Pross, who had never struck a blow in her life, was now so full of anger and excitement that tears flowed from her eyes.

Madame Defarge took the tears for a sign of weakness.

'Ha, ha,' she laughed. 'You poor thing. Look at you? I'll call that Doctor.' Then she raised her voice and called, 'Citizen Doctor! Wife of Evrémonde! Answer me, someone. Any person but this miserable woman, answer the Citizeness Defarge!'

There was no reply. A look of doubt came into her eyes. Quickly she went from door to door and looked in each room. The three rooms were empty.

'These rooms are all in disorder. They have packed their bags and gone away. Open the door behind you! Let me look inside.'

'Never,' replied Miss Pross, who understood the request as clearly as the other woman understood the answer.

'If they have gone, they can be followed and brought back,' said Madame Defarge to herself.

'But as long as you are not sure, you don't know what to do,' Miss Pross said to herself. 'And you shall not be sure, if I can prevent it. In any case, you are not going to leave this house while I have the strength to hold you.'

'I have been in the fighting from the beginning,' said Madame Defarge, 'and nothing has stopped me. I will tear you to pieces if you do not get away from that door.'

'We are alone at the top of a house,' said Miss Pross. 'We are not likely to be heard. Every minute I keep you here is worth a hundred pounds to Lucie.'

Madame Defarge rushed at the door. Miss Pross seized her round the waist and held her tight. Madame Defarge struggled and hit out, but she could not get away. Miss Pross, strengthened by love, still held on and even lifted her from the ground. Madame's hands struck and tore her face; Miss Pross put down her head, but still held on.

Soon Madame Defarge stopped striking and began to feel for her knife. 'It is under my arm,' said Miss Pross through her teeth, 'and you will not reach it. I am stronger than you, thank Heaven. I'll hold you until one of us faints or dies.'

Madame Defarge put her hands in the front of her dress. Miss Pross looked up, saw what she was touching and struck at the gun. There was a flash and a crash, and Miss Pross stood alone – half blinded by the smoke.

As the smoke cleared, it seemed to take away with it the soul of the wild woman who lay lifeless on the ground.

In her fear and terror, Miss Pross moved back from the body as far as she could, and ran down the stairs to call for help. But she remembered in time how dangerous this would be for herself, and came back. She forced herself to pass the thing that lay on the floor, and got together her hat and other things she wanted. Then she left the room and locked it behind her. She sat on the stairs for a few minutes to calm herself. Then she got up and hurried away. She pulled her hat down low to hide the marks on her face. If she had not, she could not have walked outside without being noticed and perhaps stopped.

She hurried along the streets, crossed the river and came to the church of Notre-Dame. After waiting for a few minutes she saw the welcome sight of the carriage, and Jerry looking out of the window. Even before it had stopped, the door was open and she was trying to get in. She sank back on the seat beside Jerry.

'Is there any noise in the streets?' she asked him.

'The usual noises,' Mr Cruncher replied, looking surprised by her question and by her appearance.

'I can't hear you,' said Miss Pross. 'What did you say?'

He repeated his words, but she could not hear him. Later she asked him the same question and again Jerry repeated the words.

'I can't hear anything,' she said.

'What's happened to her?' said Jerry to himself. 'How can she have lost her hearing in half an hour?'

'I feel,' said Miss Pross, 'as if there has been a flash and a crash: and that crash will be the last thing I shall ever hear.'

'Listen,' said Jerry. 'I can hear the noise of those terrible carts. Can't you hear that?'

Miss Pross saw that he was speaking to her.

'I can hear nothing at all,' she said.

'Well,' said Jerry, 'if you can't hear the noise made by those carts, now near their journey's end, it's my opinion that you'll never hear anything else in the world.'

And for the rest of her life she never did.

Chapter 27   The Guillotine

The death-carts were passing slowly along the streets of Paris. Six carts carried the day's offering to the guillotine. As the wheels turned, they seemed to force their way through the people in the streets, but those who lived there were so used to the sight that there was nobody at all in many of the windows.

Of the riders in the carts, some looked around at their last roadside with calm, uninterested eyes; some were sunk, with their heads bent, in silent misery; some, remembering how they must seem to others, gave the crowds looks of pride.

There was a guard of horsemen riding at the side of the carts, and faces were often turned up to the horsemen as people in the street asked the names of the prisoners. On the steps of a church, waiting for the coming of the carts, stood Barsad the spy. He looked into the first cart. 'Not there.' He looked into the second, 'Not there.' His face cleared as he looked into the third.

'Which is Evrémonde?' said a man behind him.

'That one. At the back there.'

'With his hand in the girl's?'

'Yes.'

'Down with Evrémonde!' cried the man. 'To the guillotine!'

'Don't say that!' begged the spy nervously.

'And why not, citizen?'

'He is going to pay the price. It will be paid in five minutes more. Let him be at peace.'

But the man continued to shout, 'Down with Evrémonde!' The face of Evrémonde was turned towards him for a moment.

Evrémonde saw the spy and the cart passed on.

The clocks struck three. In front of the guillotine, seated on chairs, were a number of women, busily knitting. On one of the chairs stood The Revenge, looking around for her friend.

'Thérèse!' she cried. 'Who has seen her? Thérèse Defarge!'

'She has never missed before,' said one of the women.

'No; nor will she miss now,' cried The Revenge. 'Thérèse!'

'Louder,' advised the woman.

Yes, louder, Revenge, much louder! But she will not hear you. Send other women to look for her: they will not find her.

'Bad luck!' cried The Revenge. 'Evrémonde will soon be killed and she is not here. See her knitting in my hand and her empty chair ready for her. What a terrible disappointment!'

The carts began to empty their loads and the guillotine began. Crash! A head was held up and the knitting women counted, 'One!' Crash! They counted 'Two!'

The man they thought was Evrémonde got down from his cart, and the dressmaker was lifted out after him. He still held her patient hand and gently placed her with her back to the crashing engine that regularly rose and fell. She looked into his face and thanked him.

'But for you, dear stranger, I would not be so calm. I am naturally faint of heart, and a poor little thing. I think you are sent from Heaven to me.'

'Or you to me,' said Sydney Carton. 'Keep your eyes on me,

dear child, and think of nothing else.'

'I mind nothing while I hold your hand. I shall mind nothing when I let it go, if they are quick.'

'They will be quick. Fear not!'

She kissed him; he kissed her; they prayed together. The little hand was not shaking as he let it go. In her face there was nothing worse than a sweet, bright patience. She went next, before him. The knitting women counted, 'Twenty-two!'

The sound of many voices; the upturning of many faces; the noise of many footsteps in the crowd; all flashed away. 'Twenty-three!'

They said of him, in the city that night, that it was the most peaceful face ever seen there.

If Carton had spoken his own thoughts, they would have been these:

'I see Barsad, Cly, Defarge, and the judges – long rows of cruel men – dying by this guillotine before it stops its present work. I see a beautiful city rising in this terrible place, and I see that gradually this evil will die away.

'I see the lives for which I lay down my life, peaceful, useful and happy, in that England which I shall see no more. I see Lucie with a son on her breast, who bears my name. I see her father, old and bent, but well and at peace.

'I see Lucie, an old woman, crying for me as she remembers this day. I see her and her husband, when their lives are over, lying side by side in their last earthly bed, and I know that each was not more honoured in the other's soul than I was in the souls of both.

'I see that child who lay on her breast and who bore my name, now grown to be a man. He is making his way along that path of life that was once mine. I see him doing so well that my name is made famous there by the light of his. I see him, the fairest of judges and most respected of men, bringing a boy with golden hair to this place – and I hear him tell the child my story in a gentle voice.

'It is a far, far better thing that I do than I have ever done; it is a far, far better rest that I go to than I have ever known.'

ACTIVITIES

Chapters 1–3

Before you read

1 Discuss what you know about:
   a the French Revolution   c the story of *A Tale of Two Cities*
   b Charles Dickens

   Then read the Introduction. What else have you learnt?

2 Look at the Word List at the back of the book. Check the meanings of unfamiliar words and then complete these phrases with the most suitable words from the list.
   a to .... a scarf   e the President of the
   b .... to succeed   .... of France
   c the .... of   f liberty, equality, ...
     management   g cigarette ....
   d a death ....   h .... of a crime

While you read

3 Complete the sentences. Write one or two words in each space.
   a Monsieur Defarge owns a .... shop.
   b Lucie, who is Dr Manette's ...., was brought up in
     ....
   c Dr Manette was a .... in the Bastille for many years.
   d Defarge used to be Dr Manette's ....
   e Dr Manette learnt to be a .... in prison.
   f Charles Darnay is accused of being a ....
   g Lucie Manette says she was on a .... with Darnay.
   h Sydney Carton looks like ....
   i The jury decides that Darnay is ....

After you read

4 What are these people's jobs or professions?
   a Jarvis Lorry   d Mr Stryver
   b Jeremy Cruncher   e Sydney Carton
   c Roger Cly   f Miss Pross

5 Answer the questions.

    a What do we learn about the people of Saint-Antoine? How do we learn this?

    b Where do Mr Lorry and Lucie take Dr Manette?

    c Which two people informed the government about Darnay's 'spying activities'?

    d Does the court believe them? Why/why not?

    e How does Carton help Darnay in court?

6 Discuss these questions.

    a Is the jury right to decide that Darnay is not guilty?

    b Why do you think Carton helps Darnay?

Chapters 4–7

Before you read

7 Answer the questions.

    a How do you think the relationship might develop between Sydney Carton and Charles Darnay?

    b What part do you think the Defarges might play in the story?

While you read

8 Number these events in the correct order, 1–8.

    a The Marquis of Evrémonde's carriage runs over a child. .....

    b Charles Darnay talks about the Tower of London. .....

    c A man hangs under the Marquis' carriage. .....

    d Carton and Darnay have a drink together. .....

    e The Marquis of Evrémonde is killed. .....

    f Carton and Stryver talk about their relationship. .....

    g Darnay and the Marquis have supper together. .....

    h Mr Lorry and Miss Pross discuss Dr Manette. .....

After you read

9 Who is speaking, and to whom? Explain the situation.

    a 'You have acted as if you like me, but I don't think you do.'

    b 'But you were always far in front and I was always far behind.'

    c 'We all know that he is not guilty of any crime. Why should he never mention it?'

d 'How do I know that you have not harmed the horses? See, give him that.'

e 'This property and France are lost to me. I give them up.'

10 Answer the questions.

    a Why doesn't Carton like Darnay?

    b Why does the doctor never mention the shoemaking time?

    c Why does the man hang on under the carriage, do you think?

    d Why does Darnay want to give up the property in France?

11 Discuss your opinions with another student.

    a What is the Doctor's reaction to Darnay's story about the Tower of London and why does he react like this?

    b Who killed the Marquis, do you think?

12 Work with another student. Imagine that you are two servants of the Marquis. Discuss your feelings about his death.

Chapters 8–10

Before you read

13 How might Charles Darnay's life change, do you think?

While you read

14 Are the sentences below true (T) or false (F)?

    a Darnay is in love with Lucie and would like to marry her.   .....

    b The Doctor asks Darnay to tell him his real name.   .....

    c Mr Stryver is very much in love with Lucie.   .....

    d Carton asks Lucie to marry him.   .....

    e The roadmender visits Defarge's wine shop.   .....

    f The Marquis's murderer was imprisoned and hanged.   .....

    g The Defarges like the King and Queen.   .....

After you read

15 Describe:

    a the Doctor's reaction when Darnay tells him about his feelings for Lucie.

    b Mr Lorry's reaction when Stryver tells him about his feelings for Lucie.

    c Lucie's reaction to Carton's words.

    d the Defarges' reaction to the roadmender's story.

16 Read the words below and answer the questions.

'If you were shown some *pretty birds* that could not fly, and were told to tear off their feathers for yourself, you would start by tearing off the finest feathers, would you not?'

   a Who is speaking, and to whom?

   b Who do the underlined words refer to?

   c What does the speaker mean by these words, do you think?

   d What do these words tell us about the character of the speaker?

17 Work with another student. Discuss these questions.

   a Why doesn't the Doctor want Darnay to tell him his real name?

   b Why are so many people in the story called 'Jacques'?

18 Imagine you are Doctor Manette. Describe your feelings when Darnay expresses his love for Lucie.

Chapters 11–14

Before you read

19 What might happen in the next chapters, do you think?

While you read

20 Number these events in the correct order, 1–9.

   a Darnay and Lucie have a child. .....

   b Defarge visits cell 105. .....

   c Defarge hears some news about Dr Manette. .....

   d Mr Lorry throws away the Doctor's shoemaking tools. .....

   e Lucie and Darnay marry. .....

   f The Evrémonde castle is burnt down. .....

   g The Doctor mends shoes for nine days. .....

   h The people enter the Bastille. .....

   i A spy visits the Defarge's wine shop. .....

After you read

21 Complete the sentences.

   a Madame Defarge puts a rose in her hair because …

   b The Doctor reacts so badly to Lucie's marriage because …

   c Mr Lorry goes to stay with the Doctor because …

d Defarge goes to cell 105 because ...

e The villagers go to Gabelle's house because …

22 Work with another student. Discuss this question.

What is Defarge looking for in cell 105, do you think?

23 Take the part of Mr Lorry and Dr Manette and, using your own words, act out the conversation in which Mr Lorry asks Dr Manette for advice about his 'friend'.

Chapters 15–17

Before you read

24 Look at the titles of Chapters 15–17 in the Contents list. What events do you think these chapters will describe?

While you read

25 Complete the sentences. Write one or two words in each space.

a The meeting place in London for rich French people is ....

b Darnay receives a letter from ....

c The writer of the letter wants Darnay to go to ....

d .... recognises Darnay as Evrémonde.

e Darnay is taken to ....

f .... and .... go to see Darnay in Paris.

g .... wants to see Lucie and her child.

h The Doctor persuades the court not to .... Darnay.

After you read

26 Answer the questions.

a Why does Mr Lorry want to go to France?

b Why does Gabelle want Darnay to come to France?

c Why do the patriots make Darnay a prisoner?

d What does 'in secret' mean?

e What position is the Doctor given in three prisons?

f What happens to the King?

27 Work with another student. Have this conversation.

    Student A: You are the Doctor. Explain why Darnay should be set free.

    Student B: You are Defarge. Explain why Darnay must remain in prison.

Chapters 18–20

Before you read

28 Do you think the Doctor will succeed in bringing Darnay back to Lucie? If so, how? If not, what do you think will happen?

While you read

29 Are the sentences below true (T) or false (F)?

    a Lucie stands on a street corner so that Darnay can see her. .....

    b She meets the roadmender and Monsieur Defarge there. .....

    c The Doctor says that Darnay will be tried at La Force prison. .....

    d The jury decides to send Darnay to the guillotine. .....

    e Darnay is arrested for a second time. .....

    f John Barsad's real name is Solomon Pross. .....

    g Carton threatens to tell the English government about Barsad. .....

    h Carton wants Barsad to help him. .....

After you read

30 Who is speaking, and to whom? Explain the situation.

    a 'He will be brought back to you in a few hours.'

    b 'I came back to try to save a citizen's life …'

    c 'Did I not tell you that I should save him?'

    d 'He is accused by the people in the Quarter of Saint-Antoine.'

    e 'After not laying eyes on you for so many years, have I found you at last?'

    f 'I tell you that an escape is impossible.'

31 Explain why Sydney Carton has power over Barsad.

32 Act out the scene in court during the questioning of Darnay. Take the parts of Darnay, Dr Manette, the President and Gabelle.

Chapters 21–23

Before you read

33 Discuss these questions. What do you think?

    a How do you think Carton wants Barsad to help him?

    b Read the words below. What is the accusation? Who is the third person who accuses him?

    '… he is accused by Citizen and Citizeness Defarge. And by one other.'

While you read

34 Circle the correct answers.

    a Barsad agrees to help *Carton reach Darnay / Darnay in prison.*

    b Carton buys some *wine / medicine.*

    c In court, Darnay is accused by *the Defarges / the Defarges and Dr Manette.*

    d A paper is read out that was written by *Monsieur Defarge / Dr Manette.*

    e The paper describes how the Doctor was taken to see *two men / a boy and girl.*

    f The child of the younger Evrémonde's wife is in fact *Carton / Darnay.*

    g The Evrémonde brothers take the Doctor to *prison / their castle.*

    h The jury decides that Darnay is *guilty / not guilty.*

    i There are two notes allowing Carton, the Doctor, Lucie and her child to *leave / remain in* Paris.

After you read

35 Complete the sentences.

    a The Evrémonde brothers take the Doctor to prison because …

    b Madame Defarge hates the Evrémondes and their family because …

    c The younger Evrémonde's wife visits the Doctor because …

    d The Doctor goes mad again because …

    e Carton says that Lucie, her child and the Doctor must leave Paris because …

36 Explain why Dr Manette wrote these words:

'And I, Alexandre Manette, lay my curse on the two brothers and on their children and grandchildren to the last of their evil race.

Chapters 24–27

Before you read

37 What is Carton's plan, do you think?

While you read

38 Complete the sentences. Write one or two words in each space.

    a Carton visits Darnay .... before he goes to the guillotine.

    b Carton asks Darnay to put on Carton's .... and ....

    c Carton puts a .... over Darnay's nose and mouth and Darnay ....

    d When the .... come in, they think Darnay is Carton.

    e Lucie, her child, Mr Lorry and .... succeed in escaping from Paris.

    f Madame Defarge wants .... and .... to die.

    g Miss Pross does not want Madame Defarge to know that Lucie has ....

    h .... and Madame Defarge fight and Madame Defarge is ....

    i Carton takes Darnay's place on the ....

    j People say that Carton looks very .... when he dies.

After you read

39 Answer the questions.

    a Why does Darnay obey Carton's instructions?

    b What does Carton remind Lucie of in the note he puts in Darnay's pocket? Why do you think he does this?

    c What does Carton ask Barsad to do with Darnay?

    d Who becomes deaf and why does this happen?

40 Imagine you are Carton. Explain why you have chosen to die in Darnay's place.

41 Work with another student. Act out the conversation between Lucie and Darnay when Darnay wakes and realises that he is safe.

Writing

42 Write a letter in which Dr Manette expresses his feelings to Charles on the evening following the second trial.

43 Imagine that you were in the crowd when Sydney Carton was killed. Write about the events of that day.

44 Write a report for a revolutionary paper of that time about the life and death of Madame Defarge.

45 Tell the main events of the story from the point of view of Mr Jarvis Lorry.

46 Write a letter from Miss Pross, in England, to her brother. The Revolution has now ended. She thanks him for his part in the escape and tells him what happened to her on that day and what has happened since.

47 Explain why you think the final lines in the book are so famous.

48 Write a description of the person who, in your opinion is the most interesting character in the novel.

49 Imagine that you are a journalist writing at the time that *A Tale of Two Cities* appears. Write about the novel for your newspaper.

50 What do you think Dickens's feelings about the French Revolution were? Give examples from the story to support your opinions.

51 Discuss, with reference to other cases you know of, whether it is realistic to believe that a person would give up their life for another in the way that Carton does for Darnay.

WORD LIST

approve (v) to believe that someone or something is acceptable

aristocrat (n) someone who belongs to the **aristocracy**, the highest social class

arrest (v) to take someone to a police station because they are believed to be guilty of a crime

ash (n) the soft grey powder that is left after something has been burned

barrel (n) a large, round, wooden container for liquids like beer

bench (n) a long seat for two or more people

carriage (n) a vehicle pulled by horses

cart (n) a vehicle with two or more wheels that is pulled by a person or a horse

committee (n) a group of people who meet regularly to do a job or make decisions

courtyard (n) an open space surrounded by walls or buildings

determined (adj) wanting to do something very much, so you will not let anyone or anything stop you

dip (v) to put something into a liquid and quickly lift it out again

evidence (n) the facts or statements that make you believe something is true

fraternity (n) a feeling of friendship among a group of people

gallows (n pl) a piece of equipment that was used in the past to kill criminals by hanging them from their necks

guillotine (n) a piece of equipment that was used in the past to kill criminals by cutting off their heads

knit (v) to make clothes out of wool using two special long sticks

liberty (n) the freedom to live your life in the way that you want to

mercy (n) kindness and a willingness to forgive

misery (n) a feeling of great unhappiness

patriot (n) someone who loves their country

procession (n) a line of people or vehicles moving slowly as part of a ceremony

republic (n) a country that has an elected government and does not have a king or queen

revolution (n) a successful attempt by a lot of people to change the political system of a country completely, usually by force

roar (n/v) a deep, loud, continuous noise

scatter (v) to run away in different directions, usually to escape danger

sentence (n/v) a punishment that a judge gives to someone who is guilty of a crime

stir (v) to make someone feel an emotion

tale (n) a story about imaginary or exciting events

trade (n) the kind of job that someone does, especially a job using their hands

Cold Mountain
Charles Frazier

Inman leaves the horrors of the American Civil War and begins
a long, dangerous home to Ada, the woman he loves. Along the
way, he witnesses great poverty, cruelty and violence. Will he ever
see Ada again? And if he does, will she recognize the man he has
become?

The Grapes of Wrath
John Steinbeck

During the Great Depression in the United States, and after the
loss of their farm in Oklahoma, the Joad family is faced with a
journey of more than one thousand miles to California in search of
a better life. Can hope defeat poverty, illness, hunger, and even
death as they follow their dream?

Great Expectations
Charles Dickens

Pip is a poor young orphan, living with his sister and her husband
Joe, a blacksmith. His life is changed forever by two very different
meetings – one with an escaped convict and one with an eccentric
old lady and the beautiful girl who lives with her. But who is the
mysterious person who leaves him a fortune?

*There are hundreds of Penguin Readers to choose from – world classics,
film adaptations, modern-day crime and adventure, short stories,
biographies, American classics, non-fiction, plays ...*

For a complete list of all Penguin Readers titles, please contact your local
Pearson Longman office or visit our website.

www.penguinreaders.com